THE FOUR GOSPELS
THROUGH AN OUTSIDE WINDOW

Also by Leslie Scrase:

THE
FOUR GOSPELS
through an outside window

- a commentary -

Leslie Scrase

UNITED WRITERS
Cornwall

UNITED WRITERS PUBLICATIONS LTD
Ailsa, Castle Gate, Penzance, Cornwall.
www.unitedwriters.co.uk

British Library Cataloguing in Publication Data:
A catalogue record for this book is
available from the British Library.

ISBN 9781852001599

Printed and bound in Great Britain by
United Writers Publications Ltd.,
Cornwall.

To a host of people whose friendship,
kindness and sheer quality has enriched
my life and helped me on my journey.

Acknowledgements

I owe a debt to many teachers and authors, most of whom would hate to think that they have contributed to the thinking behind this book.

But most of all I am indebted to Malcolm Sheppard, my publisher on this and a number of other occasions. His thoroughness, accuracy and care with my dreadful manuscripts has always been exemplary and I cannot thank him enough.

For modes of faith, let graceless zealots fight;
His can't be wrong whose life is in the right;
In faith and hope the world will disagree,
But all mankind's concern is charity.

Alexander Pope: Essay on Man

Contents

Personal Introduction

It is not too much of an over-simplification to say that I grew up with two core beliefs. The first was:

The Bible is the Word of God.

In my late teens Billy Graham came over from America. He was a gifted preacher, but if you listened to him one phrase, constantly repeated, remained with you: 'It's in the Book.'

By that time I already knew that there are many things in the book: incest, prostitution, polygamy, deceit, murder, massacre and many of these things having the approval of God! It is no wonder that my first core belief had had to be adjusted and was now:

The Bible *contains* the Word of God.

But if that is true, who is to say which bits are the Word of God and which bits are not? I learned that the Bible had to be interpreted by 'the Church inspired by the Holy Spirit'. But that raises more questions.

The Church is blessed with many fine scholars. Some of them are also very fine people. But they do not always speak with one voice. Take just one verse from the Gospels: 'You are Peter and on this rock I will build my church.'

Roman Catholic scholars and Protestant scholars interpret that very differently. Whose interpretation is 'inspired by the Holy Spirit'?

I learned to admire the quality, care and diligence of the scholars of the church – although not always their special

11

pleading. But faced with such a divided church and such a host of different interpretations, who could truthfully end his own exposition of the Word with, 'this is the Word of the Lord'?

These scholars were only men, after all. (They *were* mostly men when I was young!) Should I not trust my own reading of the Bible, my own devotion and my own interpretation?

Christians who have read my *'Unbelievers' Guide'* would probably answer 'no'! If you now read my *Four Gospels*, read the Gospels themselves and come to your own conclusions.

The second of my core beliefs as a young man was:

Jesus is both perfect man and perfect God.

That is the teaching of the Bible summed up in the Nicene Creed which we often recited in Christian worship. It is not too much to say that Jesus was my God. The Father and the Holy Spirit were only seen 'through a glass darkly' and were very much background figures in my thinking and in my worship. My devotion was for Jesus.

But the trouble with perfection is that you cannot criticise it. And the very nature of divinity means that you cannot criticise that either. Which meant that wherever I felt that Jesus deserved criticism the occasion had to be explained away and that is not very satisfactory.

The divinity of Jesus raises all sorts of other problems too, although I wasn't particularly aware of it while I was still a Christian. For example: is it really possible for someone who is God to become really and truly human just as you or I are human? Isn't it part of the nature of humanity to be fallible – something which, by definition, Jesus could not be?

I was in my forties before I finally rejected the divinity of Jesus but I still found it extremely difficult to criticise him, and even more difficult to criticise him in public, not least because so many of my family and closest friends still worshipped him.

If you DO reject the divinity and the perfection of Jesus, it is clear that Christianity as a creed, and the church as an institution, go by the board. But what is left? Now that I am in my eighties, what am I to make of Jesus? Soon after I stopped worshipping him, I stopped worshipping God altogether and became a complete atheist. Now, as I look at Jesus once more, will any sort of 'spirit' come to my assistance or shall I be left entirely to my own devices? Join me in this journey of discovery; read the Gospels with me; but come to your own conclusions.

There is one note I must add:

When I wrote my *An Unbelievers' Guide' to the Bible* I mentioned that I was working without referring to academic studies or commentaries. Some Christians picked up on this and told me that I had no right to write on the Bible without studying the work of others.

Clearly I gave the wrong impression!

For 25 years I was a student of the Bible and read both widely and deeply. Given the responsibility of lecturing on St. John's Gospel for 12 months, I read everything I could lay my hands on written about that Gospel.

However, the time comes when it is not enough just to quote authorities. You have to make up your own mind about things and come to your own conclusions. So, once again, as I have been writing this book, there have only been three of us in the room: my *Revised Standard Version New Testament*, my typewriter, and me.

Leslie Scrase – Bridport, 2013

Introduction to the First Three (Synoptic) Gospels

There is a close relationship between the first three Gospels. In due course we shall see that the fourth is very different from all of the rest.

In Christian circles it is widely believed that Mark's Gospel was the first to be written and that it may contain some of the memoirs of Simon Peter.

Both Matthew and Luke had access to Mark's Gospel and they used a great deal of material from it. It is also probable that they had access to a document of the sayings of Jesus which scholars call Q (from the German word meaning 'a source'). Both Matthew and Luke used this source which explains why, apart from the material they took from Mark, there is a good deal more that is common to both Gospels.

The chief difference between Matthew and Luke is a difference of purpose. Matthew seems to have written his book primarily for the Jews, to show them how Jesus fulfilled Old Testament prophecy and that he was their expected Messiah or Saviour, if not quite the kind of Saviour they were looking for. Luke, on the other hand, addresses his book to a specific gentile and he seems to have written his Gospel for the growing band of non-Jews who were becoming followers of Jesus.

In what follows, I keep to the order of the New Testament: Matthew, Mark, Luke and John.

I hope that it goes without saying that it is necessary to read each New Testament passage before looking at my comments. I hope that my commentary will stimulate your own thinking and help you to come to your own conclusions both about the Gospels and about Jesus.

Matthew's Gospel

Chapter One

The genealogy is fiction but does it contain hidden messages?

There are three women worth examining.

The first is Tamar, whose story is told in Genesis 38.

She was a very courageous woman who played the prostitute in order to obtain both justice and a son.

The second is Ruth, whose story is told in the book of Ruth. The significant thing about Ruth is that she was not a Jew. She was a foreigner. She was also an ancestor of King David. So much for all those Jews who were insisting on the purity of the race.

The third was Bathsheba with whom King David, Israel's ideal king, committed adultery.

Is Matthew quietly saying to us, 'Don't judge Mary too harshly just because she was unmarried when she conceived Jesus'?

Nowadays in England, few of us would. But when I was a young minister many people were still very judgemental.

But the primary purpose of this genealogy is to show that Jesus is a direct descendant of King David. The Jews believed that their Messiah would be. But all the stories of Mary conceiving by the Holy Spirit and being a pure and holy virgin undermine this claim. If Joseph was not the father of Jesus, Jesus was not descended from David.

Chapter Two: The Wise Men and Herod's response.

People often associated the birth of kings with astronomical events. Matthew tells this story to try to convince his readers from the start that Jesus was no ordinary person.

But why do those who take these stories literally never seem to be concerned with the reaction of Herod?

> 16: 'Then Herod, when he saw that he had been tricked by the wise men, was in a furious rage, and he sent and killed all the male children in Bethlehem and in all that region who were two years old or under.'

Why do Christians never ask what sort of a god could allow this to happen? Why do they never notice that from the very beginning, Jesus is associated with slaughter?

The story of his being taken into Egypt and then returning, links with the history of the Israelite tribes that went to Egypt and returned to 'the promised land' led by Moses and in the end by Joshua.

Chapter Three: John the Baptist.

Christians regard John the Baptist as a historical figure, a prophet who called the Jews to repentance and to moral lives. In the process, John is scathing in his condemnation of the religious leaders of the time – men who were probably neither better nor worse than the religious leaders of our own time.

The other purpose of John's ministry was to act as an introduction to the ministry of Jesus, whose baptism is seen as a kind of launching pad and ordination for the work he had to do. According to Matthew's Gospel 'the Spirit of God' descended on Jesus 'like a dove' and there was a 'voice from heaven' which said, 'This is my beloved Son, with whom I am well pleased.'

Was it only John the Baptist who heard the voice, apart from Jesus? It was a long time before the followers of Jesus were to claim that he was the Son of God.

I'm quite prepared to accept that there was a historical John the Baptist who called people to repentance and to moral lives, and he may even have baptised Jesus, but I regard the details of the story as fiction. The condemnation of the Sadducees and the Pharisees, a condemnation which Jesus was to take up just as wholeheartedly, seems to me way over the top. However, those who choose to become religious and moral leaders, as priests and ministers do, must not be surprised if we expect them to demonstrate exceptional qualities in their lives.

Chapter Four: The Temptations of Jesus, his first preaching and his first followers.

Jesus retired to be alone and to consider the nature of the ministry to which he felt called. It is clear that he believed himself to be endowed with supernatural powers. How should they be used?

1. To feed the multitudes?

That would bring a following for sure, but no:

'Man shall not live by bread alone, but by every word that proceeds from the mouth of God.'

Yet, according to Matthew, there were occasions when Jesus fed the multitudes.

2. To perform miracles?

That would produce a following for sure, but Jesus set his face against such a path.

Yet, even though Jesus often told people to keep quiet about what he did, the Gospels are littered with miracle stories, and there can be no doubt that many of the people who followed him did so because of the things he did rather than because of the things he said.

3. To seek political power?

The country was such a hotbed of revolutionary fervour and desire for independence from Rome that it would not have been difficult to find a following. Indeed, some of those who followed Jesus clearly hoped that he would become a political Messiah. Was Judas Iscariot one of them? But that was not the path Jesus chose. He set his face against it.

So what kind of ministry was he to follow?

Oddly enough, we are not told. The only clues lie in his answer to the first temptation and in his first preaching in Capernaum where his first message was the same as the message of John the Baptist.

His was to be a ministry proclaiming the Word of God and supremely the Word of God as it related to the Kingdom of God.

These things will be defined as the Gospel proceeds. 'The Sermon on the Mount' beginning in chapter five is the beginning of that process of definition. Here we shall see what Jesus, interpreted by his followers, meant by 'the Word of God' and the 'Kingdom of God'.

But before this he chooses his first four followers: Simon Peter and his brother Andrew, and James and his brother John, four Galilean fishermen who were to become 'fishers of men'.

Is the choice of these men a message in itself?

Jesus was a carpenter's son. His first followers were fishermen. Is he saying from the outset that his ministry is a ministry bringing the Word of God to ordinary working people? It will not be wrapped in the finery of ritual and priestly mystery, nor will it be wrapped in the obscurities of academic discourse (with footnotes). It will be a straightforward message for straightforward people.

If this IS what he is saying, we can only wonder that so much of the Church has got it all so badly wrong.

Postscript to Chapter Four

It looks as though the first preaching of Jesus was either to Gentiles (non-Jews) or, at the very least, to a congregation that included Gentiles, and this is seen as a wonderful fulfilment of a prophecy of Isaiah. Yet elsewhere in the Gospels Jesus makes a great song and dance about his message being primarily for the Jews. Are these the first intimations of disputes which were to wrack the early church when Paul began to take the mission of the church to Gentiles? The verse quoted is marvellous and bears repetition, but it does raise a very important question:

> 4:16: 'The people who sat in darkness have seen a great light, and for those who sat in the region and shadow of death, light has dawned.'

That is the kind of claim which inspires, written in language which thrills and seduces. But is it Jesus and the Christian Gospel which bring light in darkness, or is it increasing knowledge and education?

Chapters Five to Eight: The Sermon on the Mount.

The Beatitudes are often regarded as one of the high points of the Gospels. I can understand why but I am not alone when I find myself critical of them. When I wrote my book *Conversations between an Atheist and a Christian* I tried to adapt them to say things that *I* could say:

> How blest are the sorrowful when they find consolation.
> How blest are those who appreciate the world in which
> they live and the good things of life.
> How blest are those who hunger and thirst to see right
> prevail and who strive to see that it does.
> How blest are those who show mercy and whose hearts
> are pure.
> How blest are the peacemakers.

All these people will find a deep sense of satisfaction in the way they are living their lives, and an abiding contentment.

You may notice that I stop at verse 9. What about verses 10–12? There was a time, when I was a Christian minister, that I was faced with the task of closing a redundant chapel and trying to unite two Christian congregations. But there was hostility between them, as there often is between Christians in different congregations. At that time I learned what it was 'when men' (including officials within the church) revile you and persecute you and (in a kind of hate campaign) 'utter all kinds of evil against you falsely' in the local newspapers.

I chose to make no response to their lies and nastiness. The whole business was sickening and, at the time, made my life a misery. It was the unhappiest period of my life. Will my reward be in heaven? I think not.

So perhaps it is no wonder that when I read the memorable sayings in Matthew 5:13, which follow, I see no evidence that religious people qualify for them any more than any others.

> 13: 'You are the salt of the earth. . .'

Christians should especially note the 'but'.

> 14: 'You are the light of the world.

> A city set on a hill cannot be hid. . .
> Let your light so shine before men, that they may
>   see your good works and. . .

Jesus said 'give glory to God', but would it not be better to hope that if a good example is set, others may follow it?

17–20: moral laws should be followed for their own sake, not in order to 'enter the kingdom of heaven'.

21–26: Jesus puts personal relationships before worship and is right to do so:

> 'If you are offering your gift at the altar, and there remember that your brother has something against you, leave your gift there before the altar and go; first be reconciled to your brother. . .'

But in the very next verses he spoils it all:

> 'Make friends quickly with your accuser.'

Why? So that the two of you can be reconciled and become friends? Oh no:

> 'lest your accuser hand you over to the judge, and the judge to the guard, and you be put in prison; truly, I say to you, you will never get out till you have paid the last penny.'

In other words, pure self-interest; nothing to do with virtue or the restoration of decent human relationships.

27–30: A few Christians have taken these words so literally that they have mutilated themselves!

27, 28, 31, 32: These verses have led the Christian Church to become obsessed with sex and to take far too rigid a view of human relationships. Only now, when it is far too late and people have left Christian teaching far behind them, is the Church beginning to respond to the society it actually lives in and to make compromises which are at best, messy, and at worst, utterly hypocritical.

33–37: The Quakers alone have taken this seriously, and in doing so have built their own reputation for integrity and have won for all of us the right to be treated as honest, without recourse to superstition or religion.

> 'Let what you say be simply 'Yes' or 'No'.'

38–42: These verses set standards which have always been seen to be beyond all of us (even Christians!) but perhaps it is true that the higher we set our standards, the more we are likely to achieve (or is it the case that if we set our sights too high, we give up in despair?):

> 'If anyone strikes you on the right cheek, turn to him the other also; and if anyone would sue you and take your coat, let him have your cloak as well; if anyone forces you to go one mile (a Roman soldier could do this to a member of a subject race), go with him two miles.'

But what are we to make of the verse, 'Give to him who begs from you, and do not refuse him who would borrow from you'?

How useful is it to give to beggars? Straightforward giving is often counter-productive. Give to an alcoholic and he will go right away and buy another drink. We need to give thought to our giving and try to ensure that it brings benefits to those who receive it. Having said that, I do believe in generosity and in giving without strings and without any thought of reward or self-aggrandisement. 'When you give alms, do not let your left hand know what your right hand is doing.'

What about 'him who would borrow from you'? I have often had to be a borrower in my lifetime and have always been grateful to those who have taken the risk of lending money to me. Borrowing and lending involve trust, and for the lender there is always the possibility that what we lend will never come back to us – that certainly seems to be the case with books!

I think we need to be very careful about lending and it is perhaps wise never to lend unless we are prepared to write off what we have lent as a bad debt. So I'm cautious about Jesus' encouragement to lenders but I wouldn't go as far as Polonius in Shakespeare's 'Hamlet': 'Neither a borrower nor a lender be'.

Finally, Jesus says, 'Love your enemies and pray for' (or if you don't pray, seek the good of) those who persecute you. . . You must be perfect.'

As for being perfect, the most we can ever ask of people is that they do their best. That should always be our goal, 'to be the best that we can be' and to do the best that we can do. In other words, to live our best. No one can ask (or give) more than that.

None of us is perfect and the search for perfection has undone many a better man than I can ever hope to be, John Wesley among them. To command people to 'be perfect' and to demand that we 'love our enemies' is crying for the moon. Some Christians argue that Jesus was exaggerating for effect. It is an exaggeration which leads to despair.

We should try very hard not to have any enemies. And if we fail we should strive for understanding, reconciliation and forgiveness. But if these things prove impossible to achieve, at very least we should learn to live and let live.

Sadly, Jesus spoils all this by linking it with rewards. Virtue is not virtue if it is pursued for the sake of rewards. It is only virtue if it is pursued for its own sake; because it is seen as the right way to live a human life.

All of these standards set by Jesus deserve careful attention and examination. They can help us as we try to define our own standards.

The same is true of much of chapter six. Verses 1–21 portray behaviour with which we are all familiar, and they warn us against it. But Jesus is still linking generosity and devotion with rewards. He never seems to see that true virtue has no thought of recognition or reward.

In verses 9–13 Jesus provides what is now known as 'the Lord's Prayer' – and still there is the same linking of virtue and reward.

He bids us pray for our daily bread but 'daily bread' is not a gift from heaven. It is earned by honest toil.

We spoke of forgiveness in chapter five. If we can forgive those who have wronged us that will save us from bitterness and from souring our own lives. But we do not forgive in order to obtain forgiveness. We forgive, if we can, because it is the best thing we can do when we have been wronged.

As to temptation and evil: other people may tempt us to do wrong but there is no temptation unless we actually want to do wrong. If we are tempted into evil paths, we are responsible and we must accept the responsibility either for our weakness or for our sheer badness. Very few of us are forced into evil paths. We choose them, at least at the outset. And although the deeper in we go the harder it is to turn back, it is always possible. Our lives are in our own hands and we must bear the responsibility for them. Jesus is right when in verse 22 he says:

'The eye is the lamp of the body. So, if your eye is sound, your whole body will be full of light. . .'

And he is right when he says (v.24) that 'no one can serve two masters'. We cannot serve both virtue and evil at the same time. But in a quite different way and at a quite different level Jesus is completely wrong.

Sometimes we have to serve two or more masters just to make ends meet!

25–35: Worry and anxiety.

Many religious people find this passage wonderfully comforting. But is doesn't bear too close examination. It is so right in many respects and so wrong in others!

Jesus said:

> 'Therefore I tell you, do not be anxious about your life, what you shall eat or what you shall drink, nor about your body, what you shall put on. Is not life more than food, and the body more than clothing?' (v.25)

That is all very well. There is very little evidence that Jesus himself ever went short, even though throughout his ministry he was dependent upon charity. The only sign of hardship comes in 8:20 where he says, 'the Son of man has nowhere to lay his head.' Many people are less fortunate and find it tough earning enough just to put food on the table and pay for the clothes on their backs.

Jesus tells us to look at the birds, but he is wrong about them. They have to work very hard to get fed and, in bad conditions, many of them starve to death.

Yet in one respect he is right. Worry and anxiety don't help. They clog the mind and make it more difficult to think sensibly and positively about the things we can do to ensure the supply of our basic needs:

> 'Therefore do not be anxious about tomorrow, for tomorrow will be anxious for itself. Let the day's own trouble be sufficient for the day.' (v.34)

My father would come home from work and tell my mother all the things that were worrying him. Then he would sleep like a log while she lay awake worrying!

One of our daughters says that she has a kitchen drawer in which she puts all her worries, and she keeps the drawer shut!

Worry and anxiety are desperately debilitating, and hinder us when we are seeking to work out the ways in which to deal with our problems. Jesus was right about that.

Chapter Seven:

1–5: 'Judge not, that you be not judged.'

Yet casting judgement on others seems to be more common and more vicious within the three Judaic religions, Judaism, Christianity and Islam, than anywhere else in human society. Jesus himself is far from free from it.

6: 'Do not give dogs what is holy; and do not throw pearls before swine.'

Does this not involve judging people? Who am I to say of anyone else that s/he is unworthy to receive the best that I have to offer.

7–12: 'Ask, and it will be given you; seek, and you will find; knock, and it will be opened to you.'

Jesus uses this statement to claim that God will always give good things to those who ask him, because God is more generous than decent humans who will also always give good things to those who ask for them.

But even decent human beings are not always generous and kind. What is true is that if you don't ask nothing will be given most of the time; and if you don't seek you almost certainly won't find; and if you don't knock you will stand outside the door for ever unless someone happens to find you there.

13–23: Having begun this chapter by telling us not to be judgemental, the whole of the rest of the chapter is about the judgement of God and the separation of people into those who are acceptable to God and those who are not!

24–27: The famous parable of the two builders, one of whom builds on rock and the other on sand.

Modern technology has made this out of date. It is possible nowadays to build on virtually anything.

Chapter Eight: Stories of Healings.

1–4: The healing of a man with leprosy. Jesus shows himself

25

concerned that the man should go through the proper procedures after healing.

5–17: The story of the centurion and his servant is particularly attractive. Without tying ourselves to the accuracy of any of these stories, there is no need to deny the claim that Jesus was a faith healer.

But faith healing often gets in the way of scientific medicine and the Church has a long history of obstructing advance.

18–22: Jesus claims priority over our filial responsibilities.

If we all obeyed, who would care for the frail and elderly? This is far from the only time Jesus demands more than it is right for any man to give.

23–27: I once read a commentary which claimed that the meaning of this story is that Jesus brings calm wherever he is. It is a neat and comforting way to side-step the question of whether Jesus really had authority over the weather.

28–34: the story of the Gadarene swine.

For Christians this is a story about casting out demons. Non-Christians will be concerned about the swine-herds who lost their living and about the pigs which lost their lives. The fact that, in the time of Jesus, swineherds were the lowest of the low to Jews because pig-meat was unclean is irrelevant. When I discussed this on a radio programme with two Christians, they were not concerned about the swineherds or the pigs either. Neither was Jesus. But he should have been.

Chapter Nine

1–8: the healing of a paralysed man.

In this healing Jesus claimed to be able to forgive sins in the way that a priest pronounces absolution. Did Jesus know more about this man than we do? Was his paralysis due to some psychological trauma?

There are certainly times when, if people can believe in absolution, they can find peace and also sometimes healing.

10–13: Asked why he eats with tax-gatherers and sinners Jesus answers that these are the people who need him. Righteous people have no need of him.

That answer invites the question, why are so many Christian leaders so eager to be with people of wealth and power and influence and why are so few of them willing to be with the social outcasts of our time and with the poor?

From this passage we should also notice his words, 'I desire mercy and not sacrifice'.

That tiny sentence undermines the whole of the worship at the Temple in Jerusalem and also a great deal of the worship of other primitive religions.

Does it also undermine Jesus' belief that his own death was to be a sacrifice – the one perfect sacrifice?

18–26: two lovely stories about healings.

The one about Jairus' daughter is significant because Christians claim that Jesus raised her from death, yet Jesus himself said, 'the girl is not dead but sleeping.'

Once again, when I pointed this out in a radio discussion, the Christians failed to see that it mattered. But it DOES matter.

If the disciples exaggerated the facts on that occasion and made claims that were not true – claims that Jesus himself denied, how many more of the stories about Jesus are blown up out of all proportion to the facts?

Chapter Ten

1–15: Jesus had some pretty nasty things to say about those who didn't welcome his disciples when he sent them out on an evangelical mission:

16–33: the chapter continues by speaking of the divisive results which follow from the preaching of the Christian Gospel. It includes much that is memorable including:

> 'Are not two sparrows sold for a penny? And not one of them will fall to the ground without your Father's will. But even the hairs of your head are numbered. Fear not, therefore; you are of more value than many sparrows.'

This raises such a host of questions. Does God really care about each sparrow that dies? Does he care about the death toll after an earthquake or a tsunami, a hurricane or a tornado? Does he care about the grief and pain of survivors who have lost their loved ones? And if he does, why does he allow such things?

Of course, if there is no god, these moral questions do not arise. We can look at these tragedies in purely scientific terms, seek natural explanations and face human tragedy with human resources of love, compassion and support.

Finally, are we really of more value than sparrows? We are to us but not to them!

34–39: these verses are so very important to Christians but it is the first part of this passage which the rest of us notice:

> 'Do not think that I have come to bring peace on earth; I have not come to bring peace, but a sword. For I have come to set a man against his father, and a daughter against her mother, and a daughter-in-law against her mother-in-law; and a man's foes will be those of his own household.
>
> He who loves father or mother more than me is not worthy of me; and he who loves son or daughter more than me is not worthy of me.'

Those words, which have proved to be so tragically true, should be enough on their own to turn all of us away from Jesus, his Gospel and his church.

Chapter Eleven

Jesus is so full of contradictions. This chapter contains so much about woes and judgements and then Jesus says:

> 'Come to me, all who labour and are heavy-laden, and I will give you rest. Take my yoke upon you, and learn from me; for I am gentle and lowly in heart, and you will find rest for your souls. For my yoke is easy, and my burden is light.'

But after all that has gone before, these words just don't add up.

Chapter Twelve

A chapter reminding us that human need is more important than ritual law. It is a rather itsy-bitsy chapter so that my notes are itsy-bitsy too! As with the sparrows, so with sheep, most people would agree with Jesus when he says 'Of how much more value is a man than a sheep'. I doubt if many sheep would agree!

In the eyes of man that is obviously true, but if there were the God Christians claim to worship, would it be true for God?

12: 'It is lawful to do good on the sabbath.' i.e. it is ALWAYS lawful to do good.

25: We are often told that 'unity is strength'. Jesus expressed the negative of this:

> 'Every kingdom divided against itself is laid waste, and no city or house divided against itself will stand.'

21 contains the famous words 'every sin and blasphemy will be forgiven men, but the blasphemy against the Spirit will not be forgiven.'

Scholars have wrestled endlessly trying to determine what these words mean. No one seems very sure. If there really is an unforgivable sin, this seems a very strange choice.

22–42: In the midst of another dose of denunciation appears: 35: 'The good man out of his good treasure brings forth good.'

43–45: Here is a passage which will speak to anybody confronting addiction and anyone who is trying to help addicts of any kind.

However important the drying out process may be, unless something good and positive replaces the addiction, the addict will only fall back into his/her old ways and be in a worse plight than before.

46–50: One of a number of examples of Jesus treating his family badly.

Chapter Thirteen

1–9: The parable of the sower expresses fairly obvious truths about the work of any farmer, gardener or teacher. This does not prevent Jesus or Matthew from going on to speak of parables as inscrutable (v.12) and of value to only a limited number of people. Nor does it prevent an exposition of the obvious (vvs. 18–23).

But let us look at parables more generally and more positively:

It is in the nature of a parable that it is designed to make us think. There is an obvious layer of meaning – Matthew gives us the obvious layer of meaning for the parable of the sower – but if we think about the parable we shall come up with other meanings. For example:

This parable can tell us that it is important that we and our children live in a good environment, free from the 'rocks' and 'thistles', poverty or bad company that would stunt or harm our growth.

29

Whether that was in the mind of Jesus when he told the parable is questionable, but it is a legitimate and useful interpretation. People sometimes say of poetry (even of my poetry) that it is multi-layered and that we must look for other, deeper(?) meanings. I remember once speaking to a man about a picture he had painted. He asked me what I saw and I told him. My interpretation was what I saw, but it had no resemblance to what he saw when he painted it – he painted his nightmare! Yet, to me, my interpretation was valuable.

Even in my Christian days I was sometimes criticised for my interpretation of parables. The criticism may well have been justified but the central fact remains: there is always more to a parable than immediately meets the eye. It invites us to remember it and to think about it.

In verse 12 a bitter truth is expressed: 'To him who has more will be given. . . but from him who has not, even what he has will be taken away.'

Sadly, that is one of the fundamental truths of everyday life.

24–42: the parable of the wheat and tares speaks of good and bad living and growing together until the harvest. But the simple fact is that we are all of us a mixture of good and bad. There is no human being who is wholly good, nor is there one who is wholly bad. So the exposition in 36–43 is nonsense as is its final judgement on the wicked.

The rest of the chapter is full of parables about the growth of the kingdom of heaven and about its divisiveness, with condemnation for 'evil' people.

The more I read these passages of condemnation and judgement; the more I recognise the divisiveness of this Gospel; the more I find it distasteful.

Chapter Fourteen

1–12: The chapter begins with the rather sad and sordid story of the death of John the Baptist.

13–21: The feeding of the five thousand.

This is the only story included in *all four Gospels* but the record of it is inconsistent – there were obviously different versions circulating in the early church. Most people interpret it as an occasion when pilgrims shared their packed lunches – quite a miracle in itself!

The rest of the chapter has Jesus walking on the water and Peter failing to walk on the water. It was the odd, simple recognition that I didn't believe this story that led me to the recognition that I didn't believe in miracles at all and therefore not the miracles of the incarnation and resurrection. So Jesus was not divine. He was just a man. And so, at last, I began to be able to see just how fallible he was – a real man, not 'Perfect Man'. Increasingly I have recognised those imperfections without ever denying that *some* of his teaching was not only memorable but also magnificent and immensely valuable.

Chapter Fifteen

1–20: God commanded, 'Honour your father and your mother.'

Jesus condemned the pharisees and scribes for putting their religious vocation before their parents yet he called on his followers to put devotion to him before their devotion to their parents. And there are examples in the Gospels of him treating his family pretty badly. Perhaps he should have listened to his own parable of the mote in one eye and the beam in another.

However, we can welcome his stress on real purity as against ritual purity – something the more ritualistic of Christians need to take to heart.

21–28: The story about the Canaanite woman is one which brings little credit either to Jesus or his disciples, but she is brilliant both in her quick-witted response to his insults and in her determination to find healing for her daughter.

The chapter ends with another version of the feeding of the five thousand, and makes clear that FIVE thousand is another exaggeration.

Chapter Sixteen

1–12: Jesus warned his disciples against the teaching of the Pharisees and the Sadducees.

Once we realise that EVERY teacher is simply another human being like ourselves we need no warnings. Each of us is as capable as the next person of judging the quality of any teaching. We must stand on our own feet and form our own judgements, accepting what seems good to us and rejecting the rest.

This is as true of the teaching of Jesus as of any other teacher.

13–20: This is one of the most crucial passages in the whole of the New Testament.

As I shall show, it is misinterpreted quite deliberately by the Roman Catholic church but that does not alter the importance of the passage.

It shows first that Jesus' reputation as a prophet was growing and that he was rated very highly indeed – about as highly as it was possible for a Jewish prophet to be.

But his disciple Peter goes further in a great intuitive leap of faith. He calls Jesus 'the Messiah', 'the Christ', or 'the Son of the living God'. It would be interesting to know precisely what Peter meant by this claim. But what is even more significant is the fact that Jesus accepted Peter's claim as the truth. So it becomes crucial to understand what he meant.

The Messiah (some translations use 'the Christ')

For much of their history before New Testament times the Jews had been ruled by foreign states. In the time of Jesus they were ruled by the Romans. Their dream of a Messiah was the dream of someone who would liberate them from foreign rule and set them free.

The New Testament makes it very clear that Jesus was not claiming to be that kind of a Messiah. HIS claim and the Christian claim is that we are all ruled by sin and evil.

Through his own relationship with God; through his absolute perfection; and through his choice of a sacrificial death upon the cross; Jesus claims to release us from the power of sin and evil and to enable us to enter into a new personal relationship with God – we become the children of God.

Christians find that whole concept of Messiahship compelling, wonderfully appealing, inspiring and even thrilling. Once upon a time I did too. But when I was still a Christian I found that if you really think about those claims; if you dig deeper and actually examine those claims more thoroughly; then problems begin to arise. Since ceasing to be a Christian I have slowly been able to stand back and take a very different view.

I do not accept the opening premise that we are ruled by sin and evil and that therefore we need salvation. We ARE imperfect, some of us more than others, and some of us become ruled by addictions of one kind or another. But all of these things can be dealt with on the purely human plain.

Secondly, I no longer think of Jesus as perfect in any sense of that word. Even the New Testament demonstrates that he was just as fallible and frail as the rest of us.

Nor do I accept that ANY outside sacrifice can save me from my sins, errors, weaknesses, call them what you will. When we go wrong or do wrong, we are the people who have to put things right. No one else can do it for us. And if we can't put things right, at the very least we can set about putting ourselves right and becoming better people than we were.

The whole concept of Jesus as the Messiah and of salvation depends on belief in a god and in our need to be reconciled to that god. If you do not believe in gods, and I don't, the ONLY value of all of this is that it invites us to ask ourselves what sort of people we are and how we can become better as people.

The Son of God

This is perhaps the supreme claim of all the claims Jesus and/or his disciples made. What did Jesus mean when he claimed to be the Son of God?

Did he simply mean that he had the same kind of personal relationship with God that the rest of us could have as a result of his life and death? Was he simply the first of the children of God?

Or was he claiming divinity for himself?

The stories of the virgin birth claim divinity at its crudest and most basic level – 'Mary was with child' not by a man but 'by the Holy Ghost'.

Many Christians who reject the virgin birth stories still believe in the divinity of Jesus 'God from God, Light from Light, true God from true God, begotten, not made, of one Being with the Father' (from the Nicene Creed). You can't get much more specific than that.

Intellectually, the concept of Jesus as divine raises far more questions than it solves – if indeed it solves any. But if Jesus is not divine these claims are all meaningless and we begin to wonder about Jesus himself. I was going to say 'about the sanity of Jesus himself', yet in most respects he seems to be thoroughly sane.

Was he beginning to be led astray by other people's inflated views of him? For something over twenty years I knew a good man who was highly respected. Towards the end of the time I knew him he was given the freedom of the City of London and then he was knighted and became a 'Sir'. These things changed him for the worse. It didn't help that he surrounded himself with sycophantic yes men who flattered him constantly. He began to think of himself as better, more important and somehow different from the rest of us. He still wasn't a bad man but it was a sad decline from the decent, open, genuine young man I first knew.

Was Jesus the same? From the first he does seem to have been a bit special. But he surrounded himself with admirers. Did he begin to believe that all that they said about him was true and did he shut out all the criticisms that came from people like the Pharisees and the Sadducees? Was Judas Iscariot the one disciple prepared to question and criticise him?

I ask these as questions. I do not know the answers any more than anyone else does. But if Jesus really did claim to be divine, the kindest thing I can find to say about him is that he was mistaken.

If you share my view that there are no such things as gods except as the creations of human beings, then it follows that Jesus is not and was not divine.

> 18–19: 'You are Peter, and on this rock I will build my church, and the powers of death shall not prevail against it. I will give you the keys of the kingdom of heaven, and whatever you bind on earth shall be bound in heaven, and whatever you loose on earth shall be loosed in heaven.'

The Roman Catholic church claims that Peter was the first head of the church and that he became bishop of Rome. Neither claim stands up before historical inquiry.

The Roman Catholic church goes on to claim that there has been a continuous succession of bishops of Rome since Peter and each of them has been the head of the church in his time. That is also a claim without proper historical basis.

It should perhaps also be added that there have been times when the papacy was disputed between rival claimants; and there have been times when popes have been pretty awful people. Perhaps Jesus should have said to them, as he did to Peter, 'Get behind me Satan! You are a hindrance to me, for you are not on the side of God, but of men.' (16:23)

Some of the popes were not even on the side of men, but only on the side of their own aggrandisement and that of their families.

21–28: According to Matthew's Gospel, Jesus regarded this moment as seminal. He now felt able to explain to his close followers exactly what his claims would mean. We have no means of knowing how genuine all this is or how much of it is wisdom after the events, but let us assume that it is genuine:

Jesus spells out his own future. He is to suffer and to be killed. But he will triumph over death for 'on the third day' he 'will be raised' from death. And then, within the lifetime of some of his hearers, he will 'come with his angels in the glory of his Father'; he will come 'in his kingdom' and 'he will repay every man for what he has done'.

The final part of that 'prophecy' was not fulfilled. Jesus did not come again in glory during the lifetime of any of his followers. He has still not come.

Christians claim that the rest has been fulfilled. Jesus did suffer and die and, according to Christians, he did rise from death, although many thinking Christians nowadays are uncomfortable with a good deal of the Gospel accounts of resurrection. Instead of arguing for some sort of 'spiritual' resurrection, I came to the conclusion long ago that the resurrection didn't take place and also that the second coming will not take place. There is no proof either way.

Jesus uses his own forecast to call his followers to lives of self-denial and sacrifice. There are many of his followers who have lived lives of genuine nobility in the service of others and it is that fact, perhaps above all others, which gives Christianity its appeal.

But in the course of my lifetime a host of different organisations have sprung up which are not in any sense religious organisations but which give people precisely the same opportunities to devote their lives to the service of their fellows.

How we live our lives is a matter of personal choice. I remember one man telling me that he aimed to be a millionaire by the time he was thirty. Did he make it? He certainly became very wealthy. That was his choice and that was his life. He sacrificed himself in the pursuit of wealth!

Others sacrifice themselves in the service of their fellows. That is their choice. It is not a choice that will lead to material wealth. In the end, does it lead to greater personal satisfaction? Who can say? My own preference is for the second choice but I wouldn't be dogmatic about it. A wealthy man creates doors of opportunity for himself which a poorer man doesn't have. How will he use those choices?

Life is not simple and we don't have many chances to get things right.

Chapter Seventeen

1–13: **The Transfiguration.**

Whatever you make of it, this is a lovely story. Its purpose seems to be twofold:

The secondary purpose is to express the Christian claim that the prophetic ministry of John the Baptist was the fulfilment of Jewish expectations that a second Elijah would preface the arrival of the Messiah.

The first purpose is to portray Jesus as that Messiah and to underpin Peter's claim that Jesus is the Son of God.

A non-Christian cannot comment on the story without giving offence. Apart from the followers of Jesus, the Jews of the time never accepted either the claim that John the Baptist was the second Elijah or the claim that Jesus was the Messiah, let alone the Son of God. Neither do I. I did, but I don't now, and frankly I don't know what to make of this story.

Is it pure fiction? Or is it one of those occasions when, in times of heightened tension, people see things which are very real to them? I don't pretend to know but that is what I suspect.

14–21: **A boy with epilepsy.**

In the story Jesus heals a boy with epilepsy and condemns his disciples for the lack of faith which prevented them from healing the boy. Stories like this have done untold harm at two levels.

First, they leave naive Christians (of whom I was one) riddled with guilt because their own lack of faith means that they are unable to heal! I don't want to go on about this but it was something which troubled me seriously for years and I'm sure that I was not alone.

But more serious than this, the Church's concentration on faith healing led it to be obstructive when men strove to find scientific answers to illness and disease. Nor is that obstructiveness entirely a thing of the past.

Centuries before Jesus, a book was written in Greece about epilepsy, called 'the Sacred Disease'. In it the author wrote: 'It is not, in my opinion, any more divine or sacred than other diseases, but has a natural cause, and its supposed divine origin is due to man's inexperience, and to their wonder at its peculiar character.' Men 'called this illness sacred in order that their utter ignorance might not be manifest. Should the patient recover, they claim the credit but should he die they are not at all to blame, but the gods.' 'But this disease is. . . curable, no less than other illnesses. . .'

When we treat illnesses as having natural causes, then we can work to find how to deal with them, prevent them or heal them. All too often the Church has stood in the way of scientific advance.

22–23: Here is another brief prophecy of Jesus' death and resurrection. The disciples' distress shows that they were thinking of his death rather than any possibility of resurrection.

24–27: **A peculiar story about taxes.**

'Does not your teacher pay the tax?'

'Yes.'

But then Jesus asks: 'Should he have to' and answers 'No.'

His argument is that only God is entitled to claim taxes and 'God would not tax his own Son.'

Perhaps that is why the Church has always been so good at tax avoidance! You question that statement. Let me give just one example: clergy homes are not subject to the community charge.

However, Jesus did not want to give that kind of offence so he paid up – or rather, a fish paid for him! Wouldn't it be wonderful if the rest of us could find it so easy to pay our taxes.

Chapter Eighteen

1–14: The first four verses are very popular and deserve to be so. They are a call to humility. Are they also a call to innocence?

A darker mood takes over. We are warned in the strongest terms (memorable terms) against being the destroyers of the innocence of others: against leading other people astray.

Incredibly there have been a few Christians who have taken verses 8 and 9 literally and have mutilated themselves.

In verses 10–14 we are taught through the parable of the lost sheep to recognise that everyone has value and should be treated with respect. Here is teaching well worth our attention.

15–22: Although this is offered as the teaching of Jesus, it wasn't. The references to the church which didn't exist in Jesus' time make that abundantly clear. Here we have the church trying to find ways of following and working out the teaching of Jesus in practice. So we have a mixture of the teaching of Jesus and the teaching of the church. The standards set are high and worthy of our respect. Christians are encouraged to sort out personal disputes privately, person to person. If that fails, they should still aim for privacy so that they can avoid giving the person who has wronged them any trouble or unpleasantness. Only when all else fails should they go public and cut themselves off from the person with whom they are in dispute.

This standard is set so high that in verses 21 and 22 Peter asks Jesus how generous we should be in forgiving those who wrong us. His own suggestion is pretty generous but Jesus says that there should be no limit to our willingness to forgive. Jesus seems to have upheld his own standards. When he was dying on the cross he prayed, 'Father, forgive them for they know not what they do.'

Although I sometimes criticise Jesus in order to show that he was as human as the rest of us – neither perfect nor divine – the teaching of this chapter and his high standards both of teaching and of life, demonstrate that he really was a very special person and a very special teacher.

I have passed over verses 19 and 20. In spite of the fact that v.19 seems to be completely untrue, verse 20 is very popular with Christians who see it as the promise of Christ's spiritual presence in the midst of his disciples.

I was once invited to speak to a local political party meeting. When it turned out that there were only four of us there, these words were quoted to me!

23–35: This is a very vivid parable bidding us to 'do as we would be done by'.

Parables like this have given Jesus his deserved reputation as a superlative moral teacher.

Chapter Nineteen

1–12: **Marriage and divorce.**

This teaching about marriage and divorce has given Christians endless trouble and is still doing so. If it is taken literally, Jesus begins by saying that a Jewish or a Christian marriage is indissoluble:

'What therefore God has joined together, let no man put asunder.'

But then the Pharisees point out that Moses allowed a man to divorce his wife (although a wife could not divorce her husband. That inequality remained for a very long time).

Jesus said that Moses allowed divorce because of the hardness of men's hearts but God's intention was that marriage should be for life. So a chink of light breaks through. Marriage for life is now seen as an ideal, not as a law.

But having opened the window, Jesus comes pretty close to closing it again and his next words have given Christians endless trouble:

'I say to you, whoever divorces his wife, except for unchastity, and marries another, commits adultery.'

Those words do not rule out divorce but they do seem almost to rule out remarriage. However, different interpretations are possible. The church always interpreted this as meaning that, after a marriage has been consummated, divorce is only allowable in cases of unchastity. The words themselves do not require such a limited interpretation.

It is also possible to interpret the words as meaning that where there has been unchastity in the first marriage, remarriage (of the 'innocent' partner) does not involve adultery. It is all very confusing, so much so that the disciples said, 'If such is the case of a man with his wife, it is not expedient to marry.'

Jesus, like Paul after him – both of them bachelors – tended to agree and went on to talk about eunuchs and celibacy. His suggestion, followed by Paul, is that marriage is only for those who can't take celibacy – a kind of second best.

I do not propose to dwell on the way Christians have tied themselves up in knots over all of this. Throughout Christian history there has often been one law for the rich and another for the poor, and the practice of the church has involved both rank hypocrisy and plain immorality. Let me tell just one story from my own personal experience.

Many years ago a lady who was a Roman Catholic came to me. She had four children from her first marriage, was now divorced and wished to remarry. She had been to see her priest who knew both her and her children well. He said, 'If you tell me that your first marriage was never consummated I will marry you.'

'But I have four children. You know them all.'

'If you tell me that your first marriage was never consummated I will marry you.'

So the lady came to me and I conducted her second marriage.

All of these problems arise when marriage is seen as a divine institution. If it is seen as something purely human, designed for the proper ordering of society and for the protection of women and children, none of these problems arise.

The ideal of a life-long union remains and is a good one. My impression is that, in today's world, an awful lot of couples fail to try very hard to achieve it. At the first sign of difficulty they go their separate ways, failing to recognise that a marriage has to be built brick by brick. But having said that, there is no doubt that humans often get things wrong. I have done myself.

Where they do, the obvious and sensible and simple thing is to end the marriage and give people the opportunity to try again if they so wish. That is what modern Western society has done, and in its own very messy way the Christian church is trying to play catch-up and to reconcile its modern practice with its ancient teaching. The best that can be said of its dilatory clumsiness is that it is unconvincing. Marriage is a human institution and should be treated as such.

13–15 reminds us of the beginning of chapter 18 and of Jesus' call to humility and childlike innocence. How long does innocence remain in a child? How soon is it replaced with mischief (something I love in a child), and then genuine naughtiness and finally, in some children, the nastier elements of human nature? We should treasure innocence wherever it is to be found.

16–22: **What must a man do 'to have eternal life'?**

What must a man DO? Protestants have always claimed that

you cannot earn eternal life by the things you do. It is something that can only be given by God and it is given as a result of the sacrifice of Jesus on the cross, and it is only given to the one who has faith in Jesus and his sacrifice.

That is not what Jesus says! When the rich young man comes with his question, Jesus tells him to keep the ten commandments. That is the first step.

Then, when the man claims that he does, Jesus challenges him to sell all of his possessions and give the proceeds to the poor and to become a disciple. If he DOES those things he will inherit eternal life.

But for the rich young man that was a step too far. The passage raises wider questions. Is there such a thing as 'eternal life' and if there is, what is it?

Is virtue simply a matter of keeping the ten commandments? Does that not often lead to a puritanical self-righteousness?

And whatever may have been right for that particular rich young man, is it best for a rich man to give up his wealth? Is it not better for him to live modestly and simply; to go on earning his wealth; and to use it consistently for the benefit of others?

That may not be the path that rich men often choose, but it does seem to me to be a better path than the one Jesus proposed. His suggestion would have made a rich man into a poor man and brought one off relief to some other poor people. The path I suggest uses the rich man's talents and brings sustained help to the community at large.

And finally we should examine the call to follow Jesus. Following a leader is an easy option. It is a negation of human responsibility. Once we have chosen our leader we no longer have to think for ourselves. We just 'trust and obey'. That was the path Germany chose under Hitler!

Certainly, if people are going to follow a leader, it would be hard to better Jesus, and yet their understanding of what that means has led people into some pretty strange paths. That is not to deny that it has also led some people to become pretty remarkable and wonderful – I hesitate to use the word 'saint' because I am not convinced that there is any such thing!

My own (oft repeated) view is that we must grow beyond the point where we are followers of any teacher or teachers. If we are to be fully adult human beings we have to learn to stand on our own feet. Yes, we shall take a great deal from all of those teachers who seem valuable to us, and Jesus has an honourable place amongst them, but in the end our task is to find our own way to the best life we can live – to say with Martin Luther, 'here I stand. I can do no other.'

23–30: Following the visit of the wealthy young man, Jesus claims that it is exceptionally difficult for a rich man to enter the kingdom of heaven. The disciples were shocked. They had assumed that it was easier for the rich than for anybody else. They demonstrate their own human frailty as they ask what rewards they can expect for becoming disciples. Jesus promises them status beyond their wildest dreams but it sounds very much like 'pie in the sky'.

I find this whole passage rather sad. How much better it would have been to discuss the ways in which all of us, including the wealthy, can find a way of life where the good life is seen to be its own reward. 'The kingdom of heaven' is not some other-worldly paradise. As Jesus says elsewhere, it lies within us. We experience it in the warmth and contentment and satisfaction which come from living our lives as well as we can, and using our gifts as well as we can for the benefit of all those around us.

Chapter Twenty

1–16: **It's so unfair!**

A lot of Christians hate this parable. Jesus seems to approve unfair and unjust dealing. I love it! It seems to me to be one of the loveliest parables in the whole of the New Testament!

But first, before we look at the parable, let us face up to the fact that life *is* unfair. There is no escaping that fact. As a poet who simply called herself Felicity once wrote:

'It isn't fair', the children cry
when at their play. . .
'It isn't fair', we cry all through our lives. . .

Yet even as we squarely face
the cruel unfairness of it all
we know we have to find a way
to live the unfair life, and live it well.

And so to the parable – a story which always makes me think of the old dockers in east London and other major docks. Every morning they would go to the docks and stand with growing hopelessness just asking for the chance to be one of the ones chosen to work that day. So few were chosen and so many turned away. And most of the time it was the fit and strong who were chosen and the weak and the old who were turned away.

That is the situation here. The labourers agree to work for a specific wage and the strong and healthy ones are chosen. I'm sure that some of the crowd simply went home at this point. It was hopeless. But others hung on with dwindling hope through the heat of the day. And as it became clear that the farmer needed more labourers, their hope was vindicated. At least they would have something to take home – they would earn a crust.

At the end of the day all those strong, healthy workers got the pay they had agreed on. That was just and fair. They could have no grounds for complaint – but boy did they complain when they saw what the farmer did for all the other workers!

They felt that they were being unfairly treated, but the whole point of this parable is that they were wrong. The farmer was fair to them and generous to everybody else. Notice, too, how short-sighted they were. The day would come when they would be old and weak. Should they not have been glad to find the farmer generous, and in the case of those who must almost have given up hope, exceptionally generous?

But didn't they deserve a reward for hanging on all day? And wouldn't their wage have meant so much more because it was so rare? This parable makes me want to jump for joy that an employer actually saw these things and chose to look after the least of his workers as well as the strongest. We often begrudge other people their good fortune and are mouldy with jealousy and envy. We should be glad for them, genuinely glad. We should learn to 'rejoice with those who rejoice'.

17–19: Did Jesus really say these things or are they prophecy after the events?

20–28: This is a sordid little tale of petty ambition and jealousy – not the first sign of it amongst the disciples. Jesus lifts the tone with his warning in verses 26–28 reminding them that they have been called to a life of service.

29–34: The healing of two blind men.

There do seem to be people with (limited) healing gifts and Jesus seems to have been one of them, but it requires the advances of scientific medicine, and also advances in simple hygiene, to heal blindness on a global scale.

Chapter Twenty-one

1–11: **The beginning of the challenge to the authorities in Jerusalem.**

Up to this point any Christian reading my words will have been pleased to find me so often appreciative of Jesus, even if I have often also either disappointed or angered that Christian. I fear that from this point onwards I shall often cause Christians either genuine distress or else even greater anger.

They are accustomed to reading these words from the Christian point of view. For half of my life I did the same, although passages like the condemning of the fig tree always gave me pause. But if you read these passages from 'outside the box' they begin to take on a very different appearance as we shall see.

Jesus rides into Jerusalem on a donkey with the plaudits of the festival crowds in his ears – people who have largely come, as he had, from outside Jerusalem.

His ride into Jerusalem is like the old slap on your enemy's face with your gauntlet. It was a challenge to the authorities and it told them that he came as a prophet. That was his claim. But the fact that he came riding on a donkey also signalled the fact that he came in peace.

12–13: However, his first act on arrival was pretty violent and clearly pre-meditated. It was a challenge to the established order. There was justification for it. The prices set by the temple traders (who had a monopoly) WERE a rip off. But it also seems to have been pretty pointless like so many of our protests against authority. Its effects would have lasted no more than a day at most.

14–17: Calling on people to make the temple a house of prayer, Jesus now used it as the venue for his healing ministry. Since his use of the temple was unauthorised this was clearly a challenge and it caught the authorities unprepared. For the whole of that day he continued before retiring for the night to Bethany.

18–22: But now the story begins to go downhill with the sour, banal little story of the cursing of the fig-tree (used, of all things, as an example of the power of prayer!). My sympathies are all with the fig tree.

23–27: The sour note continues. Jesus seems to be in a pretty foul mood. Once again he uses the temple as the venue for his ministry – this time for his teaching ministry. But this time the authorities are ready for him and challenge him.

Imagine if I had a crowd of followers and took over part of St. Paul's Cathedral in London to push my views. It wouldn't be long before the authorities challenged me, but if I had crowd support as Jesus did, they might be pretty hamstrung for a while.

The question 'by what authority are you doing these things' is perfectly legitimate.

It was a question Jesus side-stepped, and because of the support he had from his crowd the authorities were helpless, but they would not be helpless for long. They could muster the locals!

28–32: Jesus pressed home his advantage and must have pleased the crowds by his criticisms of those in authority.

People in authority frustrate all of us sometimes whether on the national level or on the local level. We write letters to MPs or we join protest organisations or marches and none of it seems to get us very far.

So, when their frailties are revealed and we see top dogs taken down a peg or two, or even humiliated, we have little sympathy with them and tend to forget our own frailties and weaknesses.

We have every right to criticise those in authority when they do stupid things in our name or even evil things in our name. But we always need to ask ourselves if our criticisms are fair.

33–41: The sour judgemental, condemnatory mood continues, so let us stop for a moment and ask that question. Was Jesus being fair?

Ask yourselves what you think of the clergy. It is easy to criticise them and sometimes they almost seem to go out of their way to invite criticism. But whatever their faults and inadequacies they are a pretty decent bunch of people on the whole. I speak as one who belonged to their profession for twenty years!

Do we really think that the priests of Jesus' time were significantly different or significantly worse? No. Jesus is just playing to the gallery. The more I think about it the more I feel that he was unjustified in slagging off the priests of his day as he does and the same goes for his criticisms of lawyers. They are no better and no worse than the rest of us. This chapter doesn't show Jesus in a very good light at all. It is all pretty negative and sour.

We can understand that because he was filled with foreboding about his own personal immediate future and he must have been pretty depressed, but that doesn't make it right.

Sadly, all of these things have distracted us from the one really useful message in all of this which my cousin Ralphie summarised for me in a quotation he put in my childhood autograph book. The message is in verses 28–31. I like my cousin's version:

'It is better to do and not promise, than to promise and not do.'

Chapter Twenty-Two

1–14: Except for the very last verse this passage doesn't seem to me to have anything of relevance to say unless you happen to be a Jew or a Christian. The last verse would ring true for the unemployed seeking work and going to interview after interview:

'Many are called but few are chosen.'

But it doesn't help much to know that that is true. As to its religious message, if you believe it then it is thoroughly depressing unless you happen to be cock-sure enough to believe that you are one of the chosen.

15–22: A trick question reveals how quick-witted Jesus was and it is a thoroughly enjoyable story. Let me tell you another of no relevance at all!

When I was doing my National Service in the Navy there was a Sunday when I was the only Writer (clerk) on duty. I asked the Naval Commander, who was my boss, if I could go ashore to go to church (I wanted to see my girlfriend). He refused permission.

But then I saw him going ashore! So I went to see the Officer of the Day and told him that all my work was done. Please could I go ashore to church? He gave me permission and off I went and saw my girlfriend (at church, I hasten to add).

Then I caught the Liberty Boat back to my ship. Unfortunately my boss was on the same Liberty Boat. When I arrived back on board I was greeted with a message instructing me to go to the Commander's cabin. I arrived, saluted and stood to attention.

He looked at me and I waited, fearing the worst. Then he said, 'Render to Caesar the things that are Caesar's and to God the things that are God's. Dismiss.'

With a great sigh of relief I realised that I was off the hook!

23–33: The Sadducees (priests) had no belief in life after death – the idea of resurrection was a comparatively new one in Jewish circles. They tried another trick question. Jesus dealt with it comprehensively and went on to demonstrate that their kind of belief in God actually REQUIRED belief in resurrection.

His argument is very simple and straightforward and utterly convincing – IF you believe in God. But if you don't believe in God the whole passage is meaningless.

34–41: The Pharisees, who were themselves religious teachers, asked a more straightforward question? 'What is the great commandment in the law?'

The answer of Jesus has been fundamental to Christian teaching ever since and is a pinnacle of his own:

> 'You shall love the Lord your God with all your heart, and with all your soul, and with all your mind.' [And] 'You shall love your neighbour as yourself.'

There are both legitimate and nit-picking criticisms of the second of these. The only one I want to make in this commentary is that Jesus should have omitted the last two words – and I'm going to continue as if he had.

Jesus offers a very simple and noble summary of the whole vast apparatus of Jewish religious and ritual law. For religious people EVERYTHING needful is contained within those two laws.

I suspect that they would say that without the first, the second is impossible. I can understand that claim but I don't think it is true. It seems to me that the goal and principle of loving our neighbour can be ours regardless of our religious or irreligious affiliation. It would be hard to find a better goal or one that is put more simply.

42–45: The chapter ends with Jesus asking a trick question of his own. Without academic training of any kind it is clear that he was more than a match for those who wished to show him up.

47

Chapter Twenty-Three

1–12: In training in the armed forces most of us will have heard an NCO roar at some stage:

'Don't do as I do; do as I tell you.'

Jesus says, don't copy the practices of your religious teachers 'for they preach but do not practice'. But do 'practice and observe whatever they tell you'. In the light of his thoroughgoing denunciation of them and of their teaching throughout this chapter, it is amazing that he should have urged people to 'observe whatever they tell you'.

Within these verses he condemns the religious teachers for their love of show and their hunger for deference, respect and pride of place. Do Christian clergy never read this passage? Do they not love the outward show of dressing in fine and expensive clothes? Do they not love 'the place of honour at feasts, the best seats and salutations, and being called "father" by men'?

Do the words of Jesus mean nothing? 'Call no man father on earth, for you have one Father, who is in heaven.' If they ignore these words, how can they ask us to take any of the other words of Jesus seriously?

But now Jesus himself spoils his message twice over! In verses 11 and 12 he bids us choose the path of service and humility. But we are invited to choose these things not for their own sake or because this is the right path to choose but because 'whoever humbles himself will be exalted.' Jesus cannot seem to get away from the conviction that he needs to offer rewards.

But in verse 10 there is something even worse. All this talk of service and humility is prefaced by his own claim to be the one master of us all: 'the Christ'.

13–39: The rest of the chapter is a pretty comprehensive denunciation of the scribes and Pharisees as hypocrites. It makes magnificent and devastating reading but only once does it mention anything of value to us today. In verse 23 there is a brief reminder that the only religious teaching that really matters has to do with 'justice and mercy and faith.'

Of these, unbelievers will only be concerned with 'justice and mercy' but these are as important to us as to any believer.

Chapter Twenty-four: The Second Coming of Christ.

This is another chapter that makes superb and exciting reading but I can pass over it fairly quickly.

Christians of the more extreme sects love to use this chapter to warn us of the second coming and judgement just around the corner. Sometimes they provide specific dates which have to be revised. They try to frighten us into faith.

Parts of the chapter are prophecy after historical events; parts speak of the kind of horrors which humans never stop inflicting on one another; and parts speak of natural disasters.

Throughout the chapter Jesus (or his spokesperson) warns us that the time of his second coming in glory is unknown and cannot be predicted, so his disciples must live their lives in constant readiness for his arrival in clouds of glory.

In the early church the second coming was expected at any time. As the centuries have rolled by, the teaching has been put on the back burner by most Christians. Except for the constant call to people to live decent lives, this chapter has nothing to say to those of us who are not Christians other than to warn us of a judgement in which we do not believe.

Chapter Twenty-five

1–18: I know that this is only a story, a story intended to point a moral, but it still seems unkind to me to shut young women out of a wedding. Even as a Christian I felt uncomfortable with this story.

And that is the trouble with so much of the judgemental stuff in the New Testament. It separates between person and person in such a complete and unreal fashion. It separates between Christian and non-Christian and places non-Christians beyond the pale. It separates people into pure and evil as if the two categories were entirely separate and different but they are not.

None of us is wholly pure and none of us is wholly evil. We are all of us a mixture of good and bad and all the shades in between.

In THIS story the division is even more trivial. It is between the wise and the foolish. Being pretty foolish myself, my sympathies are all with the foolish.

c

14–30: This is another cruel story – the famous parable of the talents. I remember the headmaster of a secondary school saying that a school is judged by the academic successes of the most talented children. But it is the children with few talents the teachers need to focus on because they are the ones who need help if they are to make their way in life.

Jesus' story offers no help to the man with one talent. He shows himself to be an honest man even if he is a bit gormless. Yet he is 'cast out into the outer darkness' 'for to everyone who has will more be given, and from him who has not, even what he has will be taken away.'

That may be a fact of life but for Jesus to give it the stamp of approval is shameful. The efforts of every decent human being should be aimed at evening out the score. The talented should steer clear of the obscene profiteering and greed that are so evident in today's world. And we should all be striving to ensure that honest but less talented people all have enough for a decent standard of living.

31–46: Once again people are divided in an all or nothing fashion into sheep and goats – how unfair to associate goats with those worthy of rejection!

Someone once told me that I was an 'all or nothing' person. I don't know what truth there is in that but I cannot abide all or nothing judgements of other people. Nor have I any time for a Gospel which can entertain even the possibility that some 'will go away into eternal punishment.' I never could accept that idea.

However we CAN all applaud the picture of the good man or woman in verses 35–36:

'. . .for I was hungry and you gave me food, I was thirsty and you gave me drink, I was a stranger and you welcomed me, I was naked and you clothed me, I was sick and you visited me, I was in prison and you came to me.'

The Final Tragedy

Chapter Twenty-Six

We are approaching the end, and find ourselves faced with questions about money and charitable giving. The disciples grumble at the unnamed woman's wasteful extravagance when there are so many needy people around.

In a sense they are right. As Jesus said, 'You always have the poor with you.' So we always have to be conscious of their needs and thoughtful in the way we handle our surplus so that we can benefit the needy – and the richer among us also need to question the extravagance of their lifestyles when there is so much poverty around.

But such thoughtfulness can become arid and rigid and can develop a miserly, meanness of spirit of its own. There needs to remain room for the spontaneous act of generosity too. As Jesus said of the woman, 'she has done a beautiful thing to me.'

14–25: Money is still the subject. Judas took money to betray Jesus.

There is a fairly consistent suggestion in the Gospels that Judas was money-minded. If it is true it was a sad defect in his character. But I find it significant that having chosen an inner circle of twelve disciples, Jesus proved unable to retain the loyalty even of all of those.

26–29: **The Last Supper.**

The end of Jesus' life is associated with the Jewish Passover festival. But in the midst of a private passover meal in a secret location, Jesus' actions created the new Christian ritual meal known as the Eucharist (Thanksgiving) or Holy Communion.

For Christians this is one of the most significant moments in the whole of the Gospel. It has provided them with a memorable central rite, one which is infinitely adaptable – wonderfully simple yet capable of considerable elaboration.

Sadly it is Christians themselves who have made of this rite something deeply divisive so that they can't even share it with one another. Their thinking on the subject is rigid, flawed and open to ridicule.

On the Catholic wing of the church there are those who insist that there is magic and mystery in this rite so that the bread and the wine used actually become the body and blood of Christ. Carried to its logical extremes this leads to some pretty sordid and laughable behaviour amongst Christian priests, all of which obscures the fundamental meaning and purpose of the rite.

I have much more sympathy with the Protestant approach. Protestants see the bread and wine as symbols representing the body and blood of Jesus and thereby representing the sacrifice he made to bring us salvation.

Whether through the ritual of the church or through the ordinary occasions of family or fellowship meals, this is a wonderfully simple and memorable way of remembering Jesus and remembering what he thought his death was all about – achieving the forgiveness of our sins through his sacrifice upon the cross.

For Christians who believe in the resurrection and in the gift of the Holy Spirit this rite is also seen as the outward sign of their continuing communion with Jesus, their continuing experience of the Spirit of Jesus in their lives.

At its best this can be seen to be the heart of all Christian worship and devotion. It would take someone pretty insensitive to fail to see the depth and value of all this for Christians.

But those of us who are not Christians cannot just leave it there, though we may value the fellowship of a meal table just as highly as any Christian family. However, we do not believe that Jesus or anyone else can earn the forgiveness of our sins, nor do many of us believe in his God or in a heavenly kingdom.

If we have been guilty of serious wrong-doing people often do forgive us. That is one of the more remarkable and lovely facts of human life. But if we are to achieve any sort of valid inner peace or harmony it is by our own right-doing that we shall achieve it.

We carry the knowledge and memory of our wrong-doing with us but as we seek to live decent, positive, productive lives we overlay those wrongs and recover an increasing measure of self-respect.

No Saviour can do this for us but many, many people can point us in the right direction, keep us company and help us on our way.

30–35: Peter's declaration of loyalty, echoed by all the rest, is very moving and was both genuine and sincere, but the disciples were to be tested beyond their limits.

36–46: The Garden of Gethsemane

Within the inner circle of the 12 disciples there was another inner circle comprising 3 of the 4 first followers: Peter, James and John. Andrew was not included. I wonder what he felt about that? He always does seem to have been self-effacing but that seems to me to be all the more reason why he should have been included. However, he wasn't.

In his prayers in the Garden of Gethsemane Jesus sought strength for the ordeal to come. He needed the support of his closest disciples but they failed him. It was all too much for them to understand or share. They fell asleep.

In the crises of life we often do need the support of those who are closest to us, whether they understand or not. In the deepest crisis of my own life I shall always be grateful for the unobtrusive support my parents gave me. They must have been both hurt and baffled but they kept their questions and opinions to themselves, gave me their love and let me get on with finding my own way through. Yesterday I heard of some advice given to a young man: 'Always be available. Never be in the way.'

My parents managed to fulfil both suggestions.

In spite of the lack of support Jesus received, his time of prayer gave him the inner strength he needed for all that lay ahead. So much prayer seems meaningless, the mouthing of words that go nowhere. Like Claudius in Shakespeare's *Hamlet*: 'My words fly up, my thoughts remain below.'

But here in the Garden of Gethsemane we see something genuine and deeply moving. For Jesus it was a communing with his Father. For many another person in times of severe crisis there is a wrestling with torment, a communing with our inner selves, and a final discovery of hidden depths that will carry us forward. People are often astonished to discover just what inner depth and strength they have.

47–56: Like a Shakespeare play we descend from high drama to low comedy or in this case, pure bathos. We can't cope with too much Gethsemane so now we descend into pure farce with Judas' kiss, Peter's military prowess, slicing off the ear of a slave, and in the midst of all the darkness, chaos, turmoil and the flight of his disciples, Jesus, the still, calm centre in the storm.

He alone stands admirable, head and shoulders above the rest, and even still managing a memorable quote:

'. . .all who take the sword will perish by the sword.'

57–68: Before the High Priest the accusations finally focus on who Jesus claims to be: 'the Christ, the Son of God'.

Jesus acknowledges that that is who he claims to be and is condemned for blasphemy. 'He deserves death.' But under

Roman law blasphemy was not punishable by death. Some other charge would have to be found.

69–75: Meanwhile Peter plucked up the courage to be there. But when he was challenged and accused of being a disciple he denied it: 'I do not know the man.'

It was perhaps the worst day of his life. He comes across as a particularly human disciple and we feel for him; so eager, so loyal, so clumsy, so brave, such a twit and so fallible. You can't help but love the man.

Chapter Twenty-seven

1–10: Matthew tells us of the sad end of Judas. He doesn't tell us enough about Judas for us to form any judgement of the man but we feel for him nevertheless.

He regrets his betrayal. 'I have sinned in betraying innocent blood.' He brings the money he had received and then he goes out and commits suicide.

It seems to me that all of this depicts a decent man pushed beyond his limits, heartbroken and with the courage to end it all. As Brutus' wife Portia put it, 'We cannot be denied the right to die.' Judas does not deserve the treatment Christians have given him down through the centuries. At least his death had a positive result. The chief priests and elders bought a new burial ground for strangers with the money he returned to them. In doing so, they behaved honourably too.

11–14: In order to secure the death penalty the charge against Jesus has been changed from blasphemy – he claimed to be 'the Christ, the Son of God' – to inciting rebellion and committing treason – he claimed to be 'the King of the Jews'. Jesus offered no defence.

15–26: It is here that we see a different crowd in action. Jesus had been supported by the pilgrims flocking in from Galilee. But the chief priests and elders were masters of the Jerusalem crowd. When Pilate, according to custom at the Passover, offered to release a prisoner and gave the crowd the choice between a notorious prisoner called Barabbas (possibly his name was Jesus Barabbas!) and Jesus, the crowd chose Barabbas and called for the crucifixion of Jesus.

In order to keep the peace Pilate released Barabbas and gave

Jesus for crucifixion, washing his hands of the whole affair. This had nothing to do with justice. His job was to keep public order. If that took the death of an innocent man, so be it. Governments do not change.

27–31: Nor do soldiers. These behaved as soldiers so often do – badly. They treated Jesus as American and British troops have treated Iraqi and 'terrorist' prisoners in recent times. It was and is pretty sordid.

32–44: They took him out and crucified him and the nastiness and mockery continued. Human behaviour can be pretty foul at its worst.

45–54: In Matthew's Gospel there is only one cry from the cross: 'My God, my God, why hast thou forsaken me?'

This sounds like a cry of despair, the final realisation that he has allowed himself to be carried away and to believe too much about himself.

But it may not be a cry of despair and Christians certainly hope that it wasn't. The words come from the beginning of psalm 22, a fairly long psalm which ends in triumph. It is possible that Jesus is inviting his disciples to see his death, which seems to be such a final denial of all his claims, as the actual symbol of his ultimate triumph.

According to Matthew, the death of Jesus was accompanied by severe disturbances in the natural world which filled people with awe and led some to think that Jesus was a son of God after all.

55–66: Women among the followers of Jesus were there 'ministering to him' as he died and they saw what happened next. Joseph of Arimathea, a rich and influential follower of Jesus obtained permission from Pilate to bury Jesus in a tomb 'hewn in the rock'. The women watched the burial. On the following day the Jewish authorities placed a guard on the tomb and sealed it so that the disciples would not be able to remove the body.

Chapter Twenty-eight

1–15: The Resurrection

The story of the crucifixion was full of disturbances in the natural world. The same is true of the story of the resurrection but this time we have an angel of the Lord as well. The angel invites the women to look in the tomb and see that the body of Jesus is not there 'for he has risen'. And then he instructs them to tell the other disciples 'he has risen from the dead.'

Then the women actually met Jesus and 'took hold of his feet.' So this is still very much a physical resurrection.

Meanwhile the guards were in a terrible state for fear of the angel and because the body they were guarding had gone. They went to the authorities and were paid to say that the disciples had stolen the body.

What are we to make of it all?

The first thing to say is that many Christians ask the same question and have serious misgivings about the stories of the resurrection. Many of them deny a physical resurrection altogether and fall back on talk of a 'spiritual' resurrection – the word 'spiritual' covers such a host of vague thoughts and feelings safely!

Books have been written to try to explain what actually happened. When I was a young man a book called 'Who moved the stone' (by Frank Morison?) looked at all the possible explanations except perhaps one – my memory may be doing him an injustice.

It is interesting that only in the most unbelievable parts of his story does Matthew feel it is necessary to introduce angels to add conviction to his story. But what added conviction in his day now actually detracts from the story and makes it less believable. The same is true of the physical business of the women holding Jesus' feet. In Matthew's day that would have added to the belief that the story was true. Nowadays it suggests that the author is trying too hard to convince us.

What did happen and what is the truth?

Like everyone else, I must plead ignorance. I have recently been criticised for saying 'miracles don't happen, therefore the resurrection didn't happen.' I must qualify my statement. '*If* miracles don't happen, then the resurrection didn't happen.'

But if it didn't happen, what did? It is impossible to know, but do you remember those natural disturbances Matthew records both at the time of the crucifixion and at the resurrection?

In a book by the Revd Frank Pagden (who was a student at the same time as I was) he claims that the area where these events took place is on a geological fault line so that disturbances in the natural world were entirely possible.

Yet I have never heard a Christian make anything of Matthew's simple statement in 28:2, On 'the first day of the week. . . there was a great earthquake.'

If there really was an earthquake which disturbed the tomb, isn't the simplest explanation of what happened to the body of Jesus that it just fell into the earth?

16–20: The Gospel ends with a final meeting between Jesus and his disciples in Galilee and his command to them to spread his teaching throughout the world and to make disciples 'baptizing them in the name of the Father and of the Son and of the Holy Ghost'.

For both good and evil, that is what they have tried to do ever since.

COMMENT

Anyone who studies Christian theology will spend a lot of time studying the significance of the supernatural elements in the birth of Jesus and what they have to tell us about the nature of Jesus.

They will also spend a great deal of time studying the death of Jesus and its sacrificial meaning in relation to human sin and salvation.

And they will spend a lot of time studying the resurrection of Jesus and its ongoing significance for the Gospel and the life of the church.

Is it significant that in 28 chapters Matthew spends less than one and a half on the birth of Jesus, two on the death and one on the resurrection?

Matthew's first priority seems to have been the ministry of Jesus. That will also be the first priority for an unbeliever looking at Jesus. We see the birth of Jesus as an ordinary birth and we do not believe in his resurrection. We try to understand what drove Jesus to invite his own death but we do not see that it has any meaning or significance for ourselves. If Jesus is to have any impact on our lives it will come from his teaching.

This study of Matthew has surprised me. I have been amazed at how often I find myself disagreeing with Jesus, but at least I have been forced to think and to react.

That in itself is valuable. And from time to time I have felt that the teaching of Jesus is as fine as anything you can find anywhere, which means that after 2000 years he is still worth our time and effort. There are still valuable lessons to be learned from him.

Mark's Gospel

For anyone who feels like reading a whole Gospel at one sitting, Mark's is the one to choose. It was probably the first Gospel to be written and it is certainly the shortest. What is more, it is widely believed to contain the memories of the apostle Peter. Both Matthew and Luke used it extensively when they came to write their Gospels.

That last fact means that many of the things we find in Mark and Luke we have already thought about while studying Matthew. These things will need little further comment. This will become clear as soon as we look at the first chapter of Mark.

This Gospel contains no birth stories and ends with the announcement of the resurrection. There are no stories of the resurrection. Mark 16:9–20 is a later addition to the Gospel.

Chapter One

1–15: The Gospel begins with the ministry of John the Baptist, the baptism of Jesus, 'the Spirit descending on him like a dove; and a voice . . . from heaven, "Thou art my beloved Son".' (verses 10 and 11)

Growing up as a Christian I imbibed these stories and accepted them as a simple account of things that really happened. And having taken them on board, I never actually asked whether they were true. I just went on treating them as historical fact.

But when you cease to be a Christian you begin to see things differently. All sorts of things about this story just don't add up. They certainly don't fit traditional, orthodox Christian theology.

Christians claim that Jesus is divine as well as human. Charles Wesley wrote:

> *'Our God contracted to a span,*
> *Incomprehensibly made man.'*

In other words, when Jesus became a man he never ceased to be God. If that is true, he was never without the Spirit of God, nor did he ever need to be told that he was the Son of God, that he shared the nature and essence of God.

In other words, either this story has got it all wrong or Christian theology has got it all wrong; or else, the story is no more than a visual aid to inform onlookers that Jesus has the Spirit and is the Son of God. If that is what it was, then people were very slow to cotton on.

I set on one side what now seems to me to be self-evident, that if Jesus never ceased to be God, he never really was human in the sense that the rest of us are human.

Christians can't have it both ways. Either Jesus is God and not the same sort of human as the rest of us; or he was fully human with all the imperfections that implies, and not a god at all. As far as I am concerned, he was human.

16–34: Here is the call of the first disciples and the beginnings of his teaching and healing ministry.

People were amazed that he spoke and acted with such assured authority. I heard a clergyman a few days ago as he paid tribute to a man who had left school at 14. The clergyman said, 'Here was I with all my academic training but this man had so much to teach me.' As a teenager I remember listening to a farmer preaching. He spoke, not from book-learning, but from life and his message has lived with me ever since.

One of the problems with an academic education is that we come to hide behind our teachers and their spoken and written words. And scholarly treatises often become totally indigestible, littered as they are with references to previous authorities and footnotes suggesting alternative points of view.

Here was a man who spoke as if he knew what he was talking about. His illustrations were from everyday life and he spoke from the heart as well as from the mind. Although, when he needed to, he showed himself to be perfectly capable of quoting Moses and the prophets.

35–39: Every teacher needs some time to himself, time to be quiet, to think and to reflect. The religious teacher will spend at least some of that time in prayer.

40–45: The healing of a leper. The Bible knows nothing of political correctness. Nowadays we would have to say the healing of a man with leprosy! But Jesus did insist on *ritual* correctness. Verse 44: 'show yourself to the priest, and offer for your cleansing what Moses commanded.'

Was this out of any interest in ritual correctness or was it simply so that the authorities would not be able to criticise him for that kind of negligence? Probably the latter.

Chapters Two and Three

1–12: It looks very much as though this is an instance of psychosomatic illness. Once in my own ministry I experienced something similar when I was chaplain of a psychiatric hospital.

I came across a man who was the organist of a Baptist chapel. He told me that, as a young man, he had courted and married a girl who was Roman Catholic. Because he refused to become a Catholic she changed for him and joined the Baptist Church. Her priest visited the newly-weds and told them that they were not married in the sight of God and that they would go to hell.

At the time they were hurt, upset and offended but they took no notice of him and went on to have a long and happy marriage. Ultimately the wife died and was given a Baptist funeral.

After her death the words of the priest came back to haunt her husband. Could there be any truth in them? Had he consigned his lovely wife to hell? He became so distressed that he broke down and was consigned to the psychiatric hospital.

I was a young minister, perhaps a bit bumptious, arrogant and too sure of myself. I questioned him carefully and came to the conclusion that he and his wife had been lovely people and that they had had a thoroughly good Christian marriage. So I took him to the hospital chapel, denounced the wickedness of the Catholic priest and pronounced the man and his dead wife free from any sins that they had ever committed. I gave him absolution.

He wanted to believe that I had the authority to do these things and took absolution from me. Within a few days the doctors released him from hospital and sent him home.

13–17: Jesus was criticised for the company he kept and responded, 'I came not to call the righteous, but sinners.'

If members of the clergy or ministers try to follow his example they will be criticised for it. One lay official in a church I served used to love to say to me, 'He who pays the piper calls the tune.'

Sadly the church has rarely followed Jesus' lead and, with notable exceptions, has chosen to court those with wealth and influence. As a result the church has been out of touch with huge sections of the population and so irrelevant. Today, as its power, authority and significance all shrink, it is beginning to pay the price.

18–22: Jesus likens himself to a bridegroom associated with joy and he suggests that his teaching is new and fresh. This is wholly attractive.

23–3, 6: 'Is it lawful on the sabbath to do good or to harm, to save life or to kill?' Human need takes priority over the requirements of the law. 'The sabbath was made for man, not man for the sabbath.'

3, 7–12: His teachings and healings pull in the crowds and lead to his being called 'the Son of God'.

3, 13–19: He chooses the inner circle of 12 disciples, a fairly anonymous bunch, including Judas Iscariot, 'who betrayed him'.

3, 20–30: If some were calling him 'the Son of God', others were saying that he was devil-possessed. There was nothing insipid about people's reactions to him. He divided people then and sadly, he has been dividing people ever since between Christian and non-Christian but also between Christian and Christian. That is one of the greatest criticisms anyone can make of his ministry and its legacy. The 'kingdom' or 'house' he established has always been divided against itself.

Verse 29 speaks of the unforgivable sin. To my mind, the only evil that is unforgivable is evil that is gloried in, persisted in and never relinquished.

3, 31–35: I have spoken elsewhere of my disgust at the way Jesus treated his family. They remained loyal to him and deserved better from him. He should have left off what he was doing and gone to welcome them.

Chapter Four

1–20 gives us the parable of the sower and an explanation of what it all means. There is no need for me to pursue the matter further.

21–34 give further examples of the memorable nature of the teaching of Jesus.

35–41: This tells a story of Jesus sleeping through and then calming a severe storm. 'Who then is this, that even wind and sea obey him?'

After all my years away from Christianity I still find myself torn. I still have many Christian friends. So much that I say will either concern or distress them that I often find that I don't want to say anything at all.

This is a lovely story. Many Christians will feel that it is much more, both as an actual miracle and as an assurance that Jesus brings calm in the midst of the storms of life.

For me it is just a story. Miracles don't happen.

But whether through faith in Jesus or in other ways we all do need to find paths to peace of mind and heart.

Chapter Five

1–20: **The healing of the man 'with demons'.**

This is a powerful story but, as I made clear in my commentary on Matthew, there was no excuse for Jesus destroying the lives of the pigs and the livelihood of the swineherds. There is no sympathy for them, no empathy with them in the Gospels at all and many Christians demonstrate the same lack of concern.

21–43: Here are two healings, one of them of Jairus' daughter and the other of a woman healed by touching his garment. Both of them are lovely stories.

The one about the woman reveals something of the costliness of Jesus' ministry. Doing your best for people takes it out of you. I sat yesterday with an old friend whose wife had a severe stroke two and a half years ago. He made light of the fact that he has been her carer ever since but he couldn't hide that it is draining his resources and in this sense, costing him dear.

The story of Jairus' daughter shows how easily stories grow with retelling. I suspect that this is the fact behind many of the miracle stories and behind the tales of the resurrection. Jesus said that he raised Jairus' daughter from sleep. He was quite explicit: 'The child is not dead but sleeping.' But ever since then Christians have claimed that Jesus raised her from death and when I point out the words of Jesus to them, they still prefer to stick with their claim.

In the story Jesus shows himself to be a very practical healer for he 'told them to give her something to eat.'

Chapter Six

1–6: To the Protestant Christian and to the unbeliever this passage is chiefly of interest for its evidence that Jesus was part of a large family. He had four brothers and sisters in the plural too. It makes a nonsense of Roman Catholic claims that their mother was a perpetual virgin.

The whole Catholic emphasis on virginity and celibacy is sick and, as we have seen pretty often in our time, damaging and dangerous. It has nothing to do with the Christian Gospel and it certainly has nothing to do with a decent and wholesome morality.

7–29: Jesus used his disciples to further his mission and news of his doings came to Herod, which gives Mark the opportunity to tell the rather sordid story of the execution of John the Baptist who had been imprisoned for denouncing the king's marriage to his brother's wife.

30–44: The feeding of the 5,000 and the need for both Jesus and his disciples to have a break and a rest. My comments on this story in Matthew will suffice.

Well – almost! You will remember that Matthew has two stories, one with Jesus feeding five thousand and one with him feeding four thousand. I have been reading the Roman poet Prudentius, writing about 348 CE. He says that Jesus fed 'a thousand or more'!

45–52: **Jesus walking on the water – 'they thought it was a ghost'.**

Oddly enough this story has a significance for me far greater than it deserves. I was reading the story one morning and suddenly said (in my head or out loud? I've no sure recollection), 'I don't believe that'.

Christian priests and ministers look at these things and don't ask whether they believe them or not. They ask, 'What has this to say to me and to my congregation?'

With that sudden recognition that I didn't believe this story came the awareness that I didn't believe in miracles at all. It came as a wonderful release and set me on my path of escape from the straightjacket or prison house of Christian theology. It was my path to freedom.

53–56: Again and again in Mark you catch a sense of what a sensation the ministry of Jesus was.

Chapter Seven

1–23: The opposition was quick to jump on every trivial pretext for criticising Jesus and his followers. Perhaps you will think that this is true of me too! Jesus condemns them for thinking only of the outward forms and show of behaviour.

> 'This people honours God with their lips, but their heart is far from him.'

He also condemns them for special pleading which enables them to justify their failure to honour and serve their parents. This would have come rather better from someone who gave proper respect to his own family.

Some of the argument about the harmlessness of what we eat doesn't bear too close examination but Mark picks up one very significant consequence of the teaching of Jesus: 'Thus he declared all foods clean.'

Judaism is not the only religion to outlaw foods as ritually unclean. No doubt these laws have their origins in food poisoning when things went bad in hot climates. Hygiene, health warnings and proper care over food are all valuable and wise. But religions have gone too far in turning these things into laws.

By the time the Gospels were written, Christianity was beginning to move away from Judaism and the new Christians had no tradition of ritually unclean foods. Mark told them that that was fine. They had no need to adopt Jewish rules and customs. Jesus 'declared all foods clean.' But this passage is about far more than food.

Jesus condemns the opposition for their triviality in the face of genuine evil and ends by speaking of where evil comes from: 21–23.

The implication is clear. If evil comes from within us, each of us is responsible for his or her own evil and must take responsibility for it.

24–30: Do we praise Jesus for healing the girl or do we criticise him for the way he treated this poor, distressed foreigner? Perhaps both.

She, at least, had the wit to put him on his mettle and to force his hand. Good for her.

31–37: The healing of a man who was deaf and dumb. We can rejoice with those who rejoice. But do we leave it there or do we ask the bigger, deeper questions about a god who permits suffering and who, in today's world permits such uneven provision of health services.

We also need to ask more than a few questions of ourselves along the same lines.

Of course, if there is no god the RELIGIOUS question does not arise. So many problems disappear when we no longer believe in gods.

Chapter Eight

1–21: The feeding of the FOUR thousand. This is probably just a different version of the feeding of the 5,000. If so, it is a warning against taking these stories too literally.

22–26: The healing of a blind man. This is the second healing where Jesus uses his spittle. At this distance in time we can't know the facts but there is no doubt that a bit of spit can often be a useful healing agent.

27–33: This crucial passage shows the perceptions of the general public about Jesus and also how the disciples were beginning to think of him.

It leads Jesus to speak of his rejection, sufferings, death and resurrection. We have no means of knowing how accurately the words of Jesus were remembered but it seems clear that his dismal prophecies were too much for his disciples to take.

34–38: Some time ago a friend wrote to me and said, 'The trouble with you, Les, is that you are always all or nothing.'

In that respect (if it is true), if in no other, I have something in common with Jesus! In passage after passage Jesus lays it on the line that discipleship means all or nothing.

If you want to be a disciple of Jesus you have to put him first and this will involve self-denial and suffering. Anything less than a total and whole-hearted dedication to him 'for better or worse' is inadequate and Jesus is not interested. Unless we put him first we are dismissed. We must be his in 'full measure, pressed down and running over' or he will not accept us at all.

It is no wonder that so many thinking people like Nicodemus kept their distance, however they were attracted to Jesus. No one has the right to make such comprehensive demands. It is quite wrong to ask any of us to surrender our own individuality, our own minds and our own lives. We have the right to be ourselves, to think our own thoughts and to live our own lives according to our own principles and values. Our destiny is to be fully adult and a follower is never quite that.

Chapter Nine

1: This saying has led to a lot of confusion.

Was Jesus referring to the experience which follows, the Transfiguration? Or was he referring to his expectation of resurrection? It is usually assumed that it was neither of these things but to the promise of his second coming.

This led many of his early disciples to expect his second coming in their lifetime. There have been such expectations among some Christians ever since and also people who claim that he HAS come again but we never noticed!

2–8: This is a lovely story of spiritual awareness and enlightenment and also of human frailty. Poor blundering Peter can't just let it all embrace and overwhelm him. He has to speak and break the spell.

What are we to make of it all?

There ARE all sorts of human experiences beyond our present comprehension. Often we know that if we knew more or understood ourselves better we would also understand these experiences.

Jesus seems to have entered a period of greater awareness of all that lay ahead of him. Perhaps that and a need for personal re-assurance, led to this experience.

Notice that only three of the twelve accompanied him. Even within so small a group as the twelve there was an inner circle of closer, favoured disciples, three of the four who were his very first followers. But not the fourth, Andrew. I wonder why.

9–13: In the references to Elijah Jesus is thought to be speaking of John the Baptist and here again he speaks of his own resurrection. The references to resurrection are so frequent that I cannot join those sceptics who simply put this down to later disciples putting words into his mouth.

The Gospels certainly give the impression that Jesus expected to rise from the dead. Yet when he died, the grief of his disciples suggests that they still did not share that expectation. Nor do we know just what expectations Jesus had: physical and this worldly or spiritual and other worldly.

14–30: Jesus healed an epileptic boy. Two things stand out in this dramatic story. First, the little passage:

> 'If you can do anything, have pity on us and help us.'

'IF you can!' Jesus asks how anyone can possibly question his powers! 'All things are possible to him who believes.'

That prompts a rather uncertain, 'I believe, help my unbelief.'

But now look at the distress of the disciples who had tried to heal and had failed. 'Why could we not cast it out?' The obvious answer was that they had no healing powers but the answer given was that they had failed: failed in belief and failed in prayer.

That answer has caused distress to disciples down through the centuries who have asked the same question, 'Why can we not heal?' Is it lack of faith? Is it lack of prayer?

Some Christians suffer genuine distress over these things. They blame themselves when they see suffering and cannot alleviate it; sickness and cannot heal it; above all, when those close to them fall ill and die and all their anguished prayers fail to prevent it. I know because I have been there.

Wonderful though the healing ministry of Jesus seems to have been, it has left a bitter legacy.

30–37: Jesus tries to prepare his disciples for the coming crisis but they can't take it in. All that they manage to grasp is that a significant change is coming – perhaps the establishment of the new Jewish Messianic Kingdom. And so they start arguing about their places at the cabinet table. How very human and pathetic.

It leads to the lovely visual illustration that true greatness lies in the unaffected, childlike modesty of the person who is

67

genuinely unaware that s/he is anything special; and it lies in service. Something of the same message comes in the later story in John's Gospel of Jesus washing his disciples' feet.

42–50: There have been a few Christians, including one or two very significant Christian thinkers, who have taken these words literally and maimed themselves. Vivid and colourful language can be dangerous. All that Jesus is asking for is a single-minded hunger for virtue, purity and an actively good life.

The last verse of this chapter is so very significant if only because Christians have so comprehensively failed to achieve its call.

An undue, puritanical focus on Christian morality so often seems to suck the life out of people and leave them dull like a meal without seasoning.

And secondly, Christians never have been able to 'be at peace with one another,' let alone with anyone else. It is perhaps the greatest of all religious and human failures that we cannot live in peace and harmony with one another.

We cannot allow our fellows the freedom to live their lives in their own way, the freedom to be themselves. We seek to impose our own thoughts, ideas, morality, religion or politics.

It is right to SHARE our thoughts and ideas but altogether wrong to expect others slavishly to adopt them. They have thoughts and ideas too, to which we should listen. Having done our sharing we make up our own minds and go our own ways as adult, individual, thinking, feeling human beings. It will be natural for us to embrace those whose thoughts are similar to our own but that does not mean that we have a need to reject those whose ideas differ from us. In the end each one of us stands alone.

Oddly enough it is when we do stand alone, content with our own position in the world, that we are most free to acknowledge the freedom of others to stand where they stand. We make no demands of them; have no expectations of them; simply enjoy them as they are and where they are.

When other people, secure in their own position, take the same approach with us, friendships emerge which are genuinely harmonious. We really are 'at peace with one another.'

Chapter Ten

1–12: The teaching of Jesus on marriage and divorce couldn't be more specific:

Marriage unites two people so that they 'are no longer two but one.'

> 'Whoever divorces his wife and marries another commits adultery against her. And if she divorces her husband and marries another, she commits adultery.'

Mark, the oldest of the Gospels, has no let out clauses. But right from the beginning, by the time the other Gospels were written, the Church found the teaching too hard to bear and began to soften it.

If Jesus is God, as Christians claim, they have no right to tamper with his teaching. Faced with such a quandary, they are the ones who question whether these were actually the words Jesus used, or whether Jesus actually meant what he said! Yet they criticise the rest of us when we ask the same questions more widely.

This teaching about marriage has given the Church endless trouble. You would expect Jesus to make allowances for fallible human nature but he doesn't. He allows no room for the honest acknowledgement that we have got things wrong, nor does he allow those who wish to, to begin again.

If Christians were honest enough to say that they reject the teaching of Jesus we would all respect them for it. But they don't. They use all the artistry of casuistry to provide escape routes from the teaching while pretending to hold faithful to it. Their efforts often leave them looking both hypocritical and foolish.

Modern western society has rejected the teaching of Jesus so comprehensively that present day marriage is often treated with little respect. It provides an excuse for a desperately expensive period of partying but it often has no lasting value at all. The idea of working at a relationship seems foreign. The pendulum has swung irreversibly and too far.

Whether within legal contracts or informal partnerships, we need to learn to take relationships seriously and understand that they can only achieve real depth with patience, care, mutual understanding and friendship over time. Romantic love can offer a wonderful entry into such relationships but it needs to be built into something much more substantial.

13–16: Christians are right to love this brief, attractive picture of the respect and affection Jesus had for children. But how difficult it is in today's world to express a similar appreciation without being greeted by parents with suspicion and hostility. The weakness or wickedness of a few and the universal reach of a salacious media have spoiled so many of the ordinary, innocent joys we knew in my youth.

17–31: Here is a good and attractive man of whom Jesus asked too much. We honour someone like Francis of Assisi because he did what this man could not do.

Are we to regard the story as specific to this young man or as having universal significance? Did Jesus pinpoint this young man's wealth as his personal stumbling block on his path to virtue or is he saying to all of us: 'sell what you have and give to the poor and come follow me.'?

The early Christians in Jerusalem felt that this was a universal call. They tried it and soon found themselves in trouble and having to be bailed out by other Christians.

If we get rid of our wealth and give it to the poor, at best we have only replaced one lot of poor with another!

But since 'the poor' are not usually in a position to make their new-found plenty work for them, the chances are that it will not be long before they are poor again. Our giving has solved nothing.

Far better that we should regard ourselves as stewards of all that we possess. There are two ways in which stewardship will operate. One is in thoughtful generosity, giving where it will genuinely make a lasting difference. The other has been seen in this country where a few employers in the nineteenth century set about changing society, at least for their employees, providing decent homes, decent living conditions, decent wages and decent prospects. It may all have been very paternal but it is right that employers should feel a responsibility for those they employ, and that those with wealth should feel a responsibility towards society at large.

Each of us will define sufficiency and simplicity of life differently, but the path of virtue for the rich calls us to live simply and responsibly, using our wealth thoughtfully and consciously for the benefit of society as a whole.

You may have noticed that I used the word 'us'. In world terms, almost all of us in Europe and America are wealthy. The wealth of some is obscene but all of us face the challenge to use our possessions well and wisely for the benefit of society as a whole.

Sadly, Jesus links his call to discipleship with the idea of rewards. He is wrong to do so. Human virtue is only virtue when good is done for its own sake, with no thought of reward of any kind.

32–34: Jesus warns his followers of all that lies ahead. Whether he was quite as specific as this may be doubted but he certainly seems to have had genuine forebodings.

35–45: Ambitions surface once again within the apostolic band and with them, inevitable frictions and hostilities.

When we see such things within the twelve, or similar things within Christian communities today, it makes us wonder whether the teaching and influence of Jesus really achieves very much. How rarely it seems to pierce below the surface and be more than just skin deep.

Verse 45 is a crucial verse for the Christian doctrine of salvation. For many Christians it is inspirational. Others of us find the whole doctrine of salvation off-putting. And Christians themselves are hard put to it to show how the sacrifice of this life can be of benefit to anyone else. I have written more fully of this elsewhere.

46–52: I don't feel any need to comment on this story of the healing of a blind man who had faith in the power of Jesus to heal, except to be glad for the blind man.

Chapter Eleven

1–11: The entry into Jerusalem has been planned in advance. The 'colt' on which Jesus rode had already been booked. Traditionally this has been seen as the colt of a donkey, and that is important:

> entry on a donkey says, 'I come in peace';
> entry on a horse says, 'I come as a warrior king.'

But according to Mark this particular journey ends in something of a damp squib: 'he entered Jerusalem, and went into the temple; and when he had looked around at everything, as it was already late, he went out to Bethany with the twelve.'

12–14 and 20–26: **The cursing of the fig tree.**

A lecturer once went to great pains to explain to me that figs have two harvests. Jesus wasn't after figs proper; he was after the second, lesser harvest. So I shouldn't criticise Jesus the countryman for his ignorance about the harvest season.

Even if the lecturer was right it would make no difference to my fundamental criticism of Jesus, but I doubt if he was right. Mark was quite blunt: There was no fruit on the tree 'because it was not the season for figs.'

Even if we take into account the fact that Jesus was under a great deal of stress at the time, his reaction was petulant and bad-tempered. He cursed the tree.

Verses 20–26 show us the results. That poor, innocent tree withered and died. I read this story straight and without comment to someone who didn't know it. She was appalled.

'I thought he was supposed to be a healer,' she said. 'If there was something wrong with the tree, why didn't he heal it?'

Why indeed!

Instead, Jesus used the success of his curse to encourage his followers to believe in the power of faith and prayer. We should be thankful that this awful passage ends on a better note which can be compared to part of 'the Lord's Prayer':

> 26: 'And whenever you stand praying, forgive, if you have anything against anyone; so that your Father also who is in heaven may forgive you your trespasses.'

Did he recognise, I wonder, that at that moment, he was in need of forgiveness?

15–19: **The cleansing of the Temple.**

There is much more justification for his anger and his actions in the temple. The money-changers were profiteers changing ordinary currency into temple currency; and those who sold pigeons or animals for sacrifice had a monopoly. If you brought your own sacrifices, fault would be found with them – a blemish here, a weakness there, and they would be rejected as unworthy to be sacrificed in the Temple. Then you would have to buy at grossly inflated prices – and, of course, the priests took a cut from the profits. The whole thing was a scandal – on a par with the bonuses given to investment bankers.

So we can understand the anger of Jesus and the strength of his protest just as we can always understand the vigour of genuine protest against injustice and profiteering. But such protests usually achieve nothing except to get a good deal of anger out of our systems.

Jesus achieved nothing. In next to no time the traders were back. All that Jesus had done was to make himself even more unpopular with the authorities.

If there is a positive side, it aligns Jesus with other protesters down through the ages; and it certainly gave him a vivid illustration for the teaching which followed. But when things in society are wrong, it is not enough just to protest. We have to think things through and ask how we can alter society so that wrongs are righted.

27–33: 'By what authority'?

These verses are no more than verbal sparring.

People who have achieved a measure of authority within any organisation, whether through study or achievement, or just through their willingness to give their time and talents in return for a little public recognition, always hate it when someone from outside challenges that authority. And if it is someone seen to be without qualifications, their anger is all the greater.

In the introduction to my commentary on the Bible, I said that I had simply read the Bible and written down my reactions without consulting any of the scholarly authorities. A clergyman picked up on that. 'By what authority' did I dare to write a commentary on the Bible?

I can understand his feelings but if he had looked more carefully he would have seen that, although I am no scholar, I did have SOME qualifications. I trained at a theological college and studied both before that and for the next twenty years in order to preach and teach the Bible. Throughout the whole of that time, I was diligent in consulting all the authorities I could lay my hands on.

But there comes a time when you need to set the authorities on one side and to come to your own conclusions – to ask, where do I stand; what do I think; what do I believe?

One of the earliest translators of the Bible into English hoped that the day would come when every 'ploughman' would be able to read the Bible for himself. But there is no point in reading unless we reach OUR OWN understanding of the things we read.

d

Other people may give us useful guidance and help but in the critical moments of our lives we have to make our own choices and our own decisions. We have to stand as Martin Luther did: 'Here I stand. I can do no other.'

Like the old prophets, Jesus claimed that his authority came direct from God so that he had no need for priestly birth or training or for the legalistic training of the scribes and Pharisees.

Some of his teaching was sublime and is of permanent value. But his actual claim doesn't hold up. He was an extraordinarily gifted but also a flawed human being. All of us are flawed and few of us have such wonderful gifts. I certainly don't. But after a lifetime of examination of the Bible I have felt driven to make my own opinions known on no other authority than my own. Once they are in the public domain, they are there for other people to take them or leave them – just one more pebble on the beach of Bible study and reaction.

Even if you are inclined to, don't take my word for things. Read the Gospels and come to your own conclusions.

Chapter Twelve

1–12: **The parable of the vineyard.**

There is not much disguise concerning the message of this parable. Jesus (who claims to be uniquely the Son of God) is preparing for his final head-on clash with the Jewish authorities.

He claims that they have always rejected the messengers of God and their message. The servants of the parable are the Old Testament prophets culminating in John the Baptist. He himself is the Son whom they are about to reject and kill.

But God will have the last word. He will reject the Jewish authorities and all they stand for and another people will become the chosen people with Jesus at their head.

For Christians that is a wonderful parable for they believe that they are the new chosen people of God. But Moslems make the same claim with Muhammad as their divinely chosen leader.

Parables have always been seen as having both an immediate relevance and significance and also a permanent relevance. An outsider looking at both Christianity and Islam today is bound to wonder what they would make of Jesus and what he would make of them. Would he feel bound to tell this parable all over again?

13–17: Here is a lovely story of clever hypocrites beaten at their own game. But it does also invite us to think about our social responsibilities and the responsibilities of society and the state to us.

18–27: It is often forgotten that the idea of resurrection was comparatively new to the Jews. The conservative Sadducees didn't believe in it. The more radical Pharisees' predecessors were the people who had introduced the idea to Jews. Now they want to know where Jesus stands.

He answered their trick question bluntly:

When people 'rise from the dead' (not if) they. . . 'are like angels in heaven.' God is 'God of the living.'

Belief in resurrection is essential to Christianity. Paul said, 'if Christ is not risen, our faith is meaningless.'

There is no doubt that Jesus believed both in his own resurrection and in resurrection generally. He nailed his colours firmly to the mast and his belief must have been a considerable comfort and source of strength as he went forward to his own death. Although I don't share his belief, I respect him for the fact that, unlike many of his present-day followers, there is no shilly-shallying. He knew where he stood.

28–34: **The two great commandments.**

For Jesus, as for the Jews, the Law begins with total love and total devotion for the one God.

The Unity of God, the Oneness of God, was of crucial importance to them as it is to Jews and Moslems today.

The Christian doctrine of the Trinity is a brave and complex attempt to combine that same devotion to the Unity of God with utter devotion to Jesus and to the Holy Spirit. When it is claimed that the Trinity is beyond our understanding, Christians will tell us that God IS beyond our understanding – and if you believe in their God, that is perfectly acceptable.

But notice that the Law begins with 'total love and total devotion' for the one God. This Law is an all or nothing law and throughout his teaching Jesus shows us that he is an all or nothing leader. He demands complete and utter devotion. Nothing less will do.

I don't believe in his God and I don't believe in him except as a teacher, some of whose teaching is very fine.

The second law has to do with loving your neighbour, and that seems to me to have a lot that is useful to say to anybody regardless of whether they believe in gods or not.

New Testament Greek has three words for love. Here, Jesus uses the most demanding of them, agape, and in doing so he pushes us beyond the bounds of what is possible. It is right to challenge people but to ask the impossible is counter-productive. He would have done better to use the word philadelphia – brotherly or sisterly love or friendship – a manageable kind of love. And now let me take you on a diversion.

Have you ever watched masses of starlings in flight together before they settle for the night? It is a truly wonderful sight but you can't help wondering, how on earth they do that without crashing into one another?

A group of scientists, I think in Leicester but I'm not sure about that, studied the flight of starlings en masse very carefully. They came to the conclusion that every starling relates to the seven starlings nearest to it and it is that which enables them to fly in such a synchronised fashion, creating such an overwhelmingly beautiful spectacle.

A long time ago I was told that humans relate in a meaningful kind of way to about 120 people at any given time. Let us imagine for a moment that each of us obeys this second law in our relationships with those 120 – each of us relates in friendship or in brotherly or sisterly love. And, of course, they all do the same.

The transformation in human society would beggar belief. This second 'law' deserves to be set before all human beings as the most worthwhile of all ideals and goals.

35–37: After those wonderfully high flown dreams we come crashing down to earth again:

I could never understand why Jesus decided to play his opponents at their own kind of clever, clever academic argument. His words achieved precisely nothing, and he must have known that was all that they would achieve.

But as it happens, those words DO have an unfortunate significance for some of his followers!

Because the Jews continued to believe that their Messiah or Saviour was going to come from the house of their 'ideal' king David, some Christians went to great lengths to try to show that Jesus did! In Matthew's Gospel the author sets out to show that

Jesus belongs to the house of David through his step-father. He does this both in the genealogy and through the birth stories. Although he had seen Mark's Gospel, he obviously hadn't noticed that here Jesus himself says that 'the Christ' is not the son of David.

38–40: When I see the fancy dress of some of the clergy I wonder if they have ever read these words of Jesus.

41–44: **The widow's 'mite'.**

This is a lovely story about the cost of genuine generosity. It would be nice to leave it there. Real generosity is a beautiful thing. It asks for no acknowledgement or reward. It doesn't look for publicity on a television programme of 'unsung givers', let alone the award of a title like 'sir' or 'dame'. It is done quietly.

People give because they want to and they give to people or causes they care about.

The only sad thing in all of this is that so much generosity is misplaced and given to unworthy causes. It is good to be generous. It is even better if we think around our generosity very carefully and make sure that our giving is of genuine value.

Chapter Thirteen

This whole chapter is very colourful and is the kind of literature the Jews often produced in times when they were oppressed – known as apocalyptic writing. Part of it may well be prophecy after the event – that event being the fall of Jerusalem to the Roman armies in 71 CE – and part of it is prophecy that is still unfulfilled as we shall see, but let us begin on a more down to earth note.

1–2: Here we have the wonder of country folk faced with the most highly developed city they will ever see. When I was in my late teens I once took a friend of mine from North Devon to see the sights of London. I kept on losing him. He stood in wonder before all sorts of buildings I had always taken for granted!

3–8 and 9–13: Some Christian sects use passages like this to warn us of things like the Second Coming of Jesus in judgement; the end of the world and so on.

Early Christians got very excited about these things, and found belief in the Second Coming a comfort in times of persecution.

Many present day commentators feel that these things were probably written down AFTER the fall of Jerusalem and after some persecution had taken place – prophecy after the event.

14–18: When the Roman army advanced on Jerusalem the Christian community *did* evacuate the city – something which didn't add to their popularity among the Jews.

19–23: Christians are warned of false Christs emerging. I once read that there were 64 of them between the death of Jesus and the fall of Jerusalem.

24–27: But Christians ARE to remain alert for the genuine return of Jesus. They have had a long wait and few of them now have any real expectation of a Second Coming.

28: Forgive me for referring back to the cursing of the fig tree. This verse shows that it wasn't ignorance that led Jesus astray but irritation or bad temper in a time of personal stress, natural enough for a human being but not for a PERFECT one.

29–37: The Second Coming was expected within the lifetime of the author. 'This generation will not pass away before all these things take place.' 'Heaven and earth will pass away, but my words will not pass away.' Even though the precise time (v. 32) was not known, that was the firm expectation. But it didn't happen and still hasn't happened.

Many Christians and all of us who are not Christian feel confident that it never will.

Chapter Fourteen

1–9: **The anointing at Bethany.**

There are a number of lovely things about this passage. The first is that Jesus was in the house of 'Simon the leper'.

Nowadays we would be discouraged by the politically correct from calling Simon a leper. He was a MAN with leprosy. Either way, Jesus was in his house. The fact of Simon's leprosy does not make him a pariah or even someone to be avoided on health grounds. But oddly enough, Jesus makes no move to heal him either.

The focus on the story is the love and generosity displayed by the unnamed woman who anointed him with expensive oils. It is also on the sour grapes of some of the disciples.

They felt that our generosity should be a cold, considered

rational thing. The trouble with that is that the mind can frequently find good reasons for not being generous and for not giving at all!

Irrational, emotional, loving generosity may not be as well directed and may not achieve as much but it is a beautiful thing to see, and if you are on the receiving end, a beautiful thing to experience too.

But that doesn't alter the fact that we 'always have the poor with' us, and that requires two things from us: the first is our own generosity towards the poor; and the second and more important is a steady determination to work towards a day when poverty will be a thing of the past, both at home and abroad.

10: Christians find it hard to understand how Judas or anyone else could possibly turn against Jesus. They often associate Judas (on scanty evidence) with greed. Was he one of the sour grapes disciples of verses 1–9? Was he betraying Jesus for the money?

It seems to me much more serious than that. Judas clearly had expectations of Jesus which Jesus didn't fulfil.

But I find myself looking at this the other way round. Jesus chose Judas to be one of the 12, and 12 is not a very large number. If Judas had the wrong expectations, Jesus had plenty of time to put him right – yet he failed.

You can say that this was Judas' fault and you can say that it only goes to show that God does not compel us or bully us into discipleship. But that still doesn't alter the fact that Jesus failed with one of the twelve.

To fail to win over the religious and political authorities is never a surprise. They are so often so sure that they are right and everyone else is wrong. But to fail to win over a man sufficiently attracted to him to become one of the twelve really is a serious and significant failure.

12–25: **The Last Supper.**

In academic circles there is considerable debate as to whether the Last Supper actually was a Jewish Passover meal. For our purposes, it doesn't matter.

Verses 12–16 show that Jesus has made preparations for this meal and also that he wants it to be a very private affair.

In verses 17–21 he speaks of a traitor in the midst but his words to the traitor show no understanding of the emotional turmoil, distress and suffering Judas must have been going through. They are simply very unpleasant words of dismissal:

'Woe to that man. . . It would have been better for that man if he had never been born.'

22–25: Here is the simple basis for the central rite of Christian worship. You would think that it would be something that united all Christians but it has been the opposite.

Is it a simple fellowship meal where Christians get together to express their love for Jesus and to remember and experience his love for them? Or is it a religious rite surrounded by strict rules and regulations; governed by a rigid theology and bathed in mystery?

If it is the latter, can anyone conduct it or only those who have been especially appointed (ordained); and can anyone partake or only those who have been especially approved by membership of the (right part of the) church?

These things seem worlds away from the simple account in Mark's Gospel of the Last Supper. They are answered by different Christians in a host of differing ways and make a mockery both of the unity of the church and of the reality of the fellowship of Christians. But there is even more and worse to come.

Christians cannot even agree about the meaning of the central words of their central rite:

of the bread: 'This is my body';
of the wine: 'This is my blood.'

At one extreme Christians claim that in their central rite the bread and the wine miraculously actually become the body and blood of Jesus sacrificed for them. Many other Christians deny this and simply say that the bread and wine *represent* the body and blood of Christ.

We might think that such differences are unimportant, but it is on such differences of interpretation that separation between the varying Christian denominations is built. What should have been a lovely, simple, unifying act of love, fellowship and remembrance, (more if you believe in the resurrection of Jesus,) has become one of the supreme stumbling blocks dividing Christian from Christian and keeping them in separate and often hostile camps.

26–31: Jesus warns his disciples that they will all let him

down. What I have just been writing about shows just how right he was, but he was speaking of the immediate situation. His words prompted Peter to express his own undying loyalty – something which, within a few hours, made his own failure all the more bitter.

32–42: **The Garden of Gethsemane.**

The stress of these last few days has been too much even for the closest of his disciples and they fail to keep watch with Jesus as he endures the beginning of his final agony.

The reality and the genuine nature of that agony is plain to see. Through it Jesus derives inner strength to sustain him throughout the finale to come. (Readers of the Old Testament will perhaps be reminded of Jacob wrestling with the angel of God before going forward to his crucial meeting with his brother.)

Faced with all that Jesus was going through, I find myself torn. I do not doubt the reality of his struggle or his conviction that he was doing what he had to do. But if this agony was genuine (as it clearly was) it makes a nonsense of the Christian theology of the divinity of Christ and the unity of the Godhead.

I have also come to the conclusion (after wrestling with this for many years) that Jesus was wrong in believing that he had to die; and that his followers are wrong in many of the things they believe about that death.

43–50: After the agony of Gethsemane we descend into bathos: the betrayal with a kiss; the disciple drawing a sword and only succeeding in cutting off the ear of a slave of the high priest; and the flight of all the disciples – except one:

51: 'and a young man followed him'.

Many commentators have wondered about this verse and have come to the conclusion that it is the author's way of saying, 'I was there.' It is an attractive possibility.

53–65: **Jesus before the Jewish Council.**

The Jewish leaders were faced with a problem. They wanted Jesus dead and to their way of thinking he deserved to die for blasphemy. He claimed to be the Christ – the Jewish Messiah – and his words 'you will see the Son of man sitting at the right hand of Power, and coming with the clouds of heaven' will have shocked and appalled them.

To them, that was blasphemy deserving death, but only the Roman authorities could sentence a man to death and they didn't recognise blasphemy as a capital offence. Some other charge had to be found.

66–72: Meanwhile Peter was busy fulfilling the prophecy of Jesus that he would fail in discipleship. He was one of the very few disciples who had plucked up enough courage to see what was happening to his Master, but when he was challenged as a disciple he denied it again and again.

For me he is one of the most human of all the characters in the Gospels, or indeed in the whole New Testament: impetuous, devoted, inspired, foolish, brave, emotional, loyal, fallible, honest and because of all these things, very, very loveable.

Chapter Fifteen

1–5: The Jewish authorities brought Jesus before the Roman procurator Pontius Pilate and overcame their problem by charging Jesus with claiming to be the King of the Jews – a political matter rather than a religious one.

6–15: There was a custom at the Passover feast for the Romans to release one prisoner. The choice Pilate gave may have been more ironic than appears. There is a tradition that Barabbas was actually called Jesus Barabbas (Jesus was quite a common name). If so, we can imagine Pilate asking, 'Do you want me to release this Jesus or this one?'

The crowd was one controlled by the Jewish authorities. It is easy enough. We have seen similar things on TV in all the recent revolts in the Middle East. ANY government can soon whip up a crowd of supporters if it wants to. So the crowd called for the release of Barabbas and the crucifixion of Jesus. They were given what they asked for.

16–20: The mockery of soldiers is not surprising. In recent years we have seen both British and American troops abusing their power in disgusting and degrading ways.

21–32: In this whole chapter Mark tells the story of the crucifixion in an understated way with a minimum of fuss. He shows a weakened Jesus needing the help of the conscripted Simon of Cyrene in carrying the cross; and he shows the sheer ordinary human nastiness of the mockery when Jesus was on the cross.

It all sounds very simple as an account of the sordid end of a fine life. But there is more to come.

33–39: By the time Jesus cried 'My God, my God, why hast thou forsaken me?' his speech was obviously going so we can't really be certain of what he said. 'Some of the bystanders' thought he was 'calling Elijah.'

As we saw when we read Matthew, if those WERE his actual words, they could have been a quotation from psalm 22, a psalm which ends triumphantly. For Christians, the possibility is a real comfort.

But of course, the words could have been a very real human cry of despair, a cry that is difficult to equate with the Christian teaching that Jesus is 'God of God'.

37–41: If you grow up in a Christian family you are conditioned into assuming that because these things are in the Gospel, they really happened. But did they?

Was 'the curtain of the temple torn in two, from top to bottom' signifying the end of the old religion and the beginning of the new?

Were the women 'looking on from afar' close enough to hear the centurion say, 'Truly this man was a son of God.'

There is no means of knowing – nor does it really make much difference whether they are true or not, except that Christians would be delighted by this final sign of the respect Jesus inspired even on the cross.

42–47: A straightforward account of the burial of Jesus in a tomb provided by Joseph of Arimathaea.

Chapter Sixteen

1–8: **The Resurrection.**

Here is the simplest and most straightforward account there is of the resurrection. Women go to the tomb hoping to anoint the body and worried about how they are going to get into the tomb. They find it empty except for a young man, who is transformed into one or two angels in two of the other Gospels. The young man tells them, 'He has risen, he is not here. . . go, tell his disciples and Peter that he is going before you to Galilee; there you will see him, as he told you.'

Why 'his disciples AND Peter?' Had Peter forfeited the right to be called a disciple by his failures, or is this actually Peter suggesting that he felt he had forfeited that right?

And why did the women not do as they were told? 'They said nothing to anyone.' (Pretty exceptional women!)

Unless something has been lost, that is where the Gospel ended originally. Biblical scholars are confident that the remaining verses were added later. They tell us, in brief, things that are told us in one or more of the other Gospels and they take the story through to the Ascension. So it is clear that someone in the early church found Mark's ending inadequate.

If we stop at verse 8 we simply have the bare announcement that Jesus is risen (and that no one was told of it!). The resurrection was to become one of the twin pillars of the Christian faith. Many present day Christians have considerable difficulty with it and go to considerable lengths to produce a definition of resurrection which they can live with. I used to believe in a simple and uncomplicated way and now I do not believe at all, which is even more simple and uncomplicated.

9–11: An appearance to Mary Magdalene.

12–13: An appearance to two of them walking in the country – a story we shall find embroidered in Luke's Gospel.

14–18: An appearance to the eleven apostles with the command to 'preach the Gospel to the whole creation'.

This passage contains 'signs' taken from later missionary stories, some of which appear later in the New Testament. Already verse 16 is beginning to depict an ordered, structured organisation and an unpleasant human divide:

'He who believes and is baptised will be saved; and he who does not believe will be condemned.'

When you get down to fundamentals, that Christian message is thoroughly unpleasant. In the course of my lifetime I have met a huge number of very pleasant people. I have also met one or two fairly unpleasant characters, people I felt deserved my pretty forceful criticism – yes, condemnation even, but only condemnation at that time and for the evil I perceived. I have NEVER felt that I could condemn anyone finally and permanently, but that is what Christianity has always done, even if some Christians today are rather quieter on the condemnation front and rather more inclined to think that their God ought at very least to be as kind and decent and loving as they are.

84

19–20: **The Ascension.**

These verses tell us that Jesus 'was taken up into heaven, and sat down at the right hand of God.'

How can anybody say that? I grew up saying it and reading it over and over again without ever really thinking about it.

Jesus may or may not have told his disciples that that was what he was going to do, but NOBODY can truthfully say that is what actually happened.

Those of us who were brought up as Christians need to stop and think about the things the Gospels actually say.

And suppose the Gospel is right and that IS what actually happened, what does that do to the Christian claim that they uphold the Unity of God. Artists have painted this endlessly and there is their imagined old man God, and there at his right hand is someone else – Jesus. That is the picture this verse paints but Christian theology claims something quite different. Are we to believe the Gospel or early Christians theologians – or perhaps, neither of them.

Luke's Gospel

Chapter One

1–4: Luke stresses the fact that he was far from being the first person to write about the ministry of Jesus. Many have already compiled 'a narrative of the things which have been accomplished among us just as they were delivered to us by those who FROM THE BEGINNING were eyewitnesses.'

He is anxious that Theophilus (to whom his Gospel is directed) should know that this account is reliable. Not only has it come down from eyewitnesses but Luke himself has 'followed all things closely for some time past'. (No one has ever been able to find anything about Theophilus.) So Luke has tried very hard to ensure that his account contains 'the truth concerning the things of which you have been informed.'

It seems to me that we should respect that. As I have looked at the Gospels so far I have focussed entirely on what has been written. In particular, I have treated the reported words and actions of Jesus as if they really were his words and actions, but I'm not entirely happy that I am being fair to him in doing so.

The Gospel writers stood in relation to Jesus much as people today stand in relation to the Second World War! There are still some of us who remember that war. Here in England some of us will remember a few of the words of Winston Churchill and rather more of the words of the songs of the time. But all of us will have different memories. Imagine

Gospel writers drawing separately on the memories of the members of my own family.

My eldest brother served in the RAF flying in Mosquitoes over Europe and then serving in North Africa. My second brother died young following an illness caught while he was in training in South Africa, so no one could ask him about the war. My third brother ended up in the Army in India and in Burma. My sister and I were evacuees and saw very little of the reality, the pain and the cost of war. So each of us would have a completely different story to tell. I have, in fact, told my own story in two novels called *An Evacuee* and *A Prized Pupil!* Why novels? Because I dared not entirely trust my memory.

Of course, anyone can check my family's wartime memory against the written records of the time. Luke claims that the Gospel writers could do the same. And there is certainly clear evidence that both Luke and the author of Matthew's Gospel used two of the same sources. One of those sources was Mark's Gospel and the other was a collection of the sayings of Jesus. Their use of these two sources has resulted in the close similarities between the first three Gospels.

But the truth is that we have no real means of knowing just how accurate the Gospel record is, especially as it has not just been handed down by eyewitnesses, but also by preachers who can quite unconsciously tinker with precise wording as can be seen by comparing Luke's Beatitudes with Matthew's.

Except where obvious questions emerge, I shall continue to treat the words and actions of Jesus as if they are reported accurately. But I AM conscious that this may not always be fair to him.

5–25: Luke tells us that John the Baptist and Jesus were both born 'in the days of Herod, king of Judea'. Herod reigned from 40–4 BCE, so Jesus had been born by 4 BCE which means that all the millenium stuff put out by the Christian churches was simply dishonest. . . 'The truth' Luke begins with comprises a series of stories, beautifully told but not by any stretch of the imagination factual history. Here are stories that are found nowhere else, stories that cannot be verified; stories of an angel and signs and wonders.

They begin with the promise of the birth of John the Baptist and a description of what he will be like when he is an adult (easy enough to provide AFTER his adult life), and the pregnancy of his mother Elizabeth follows.

It is very easy to be seduced by the beauty of these stories. Nobody knows whether there is anything factual buried in them at all.

26–35: Now the angel Gabriel tells Mary, who is betrothed to Joseph, that she 'will conceive. . . and bear a son' who is to be called Jesus. Joseph will play no part in the child's conception. 'The Holy Spirit will come upon you, and the power of the Most High will overshadow you. Therefore the child to be born will be called holy, the Son of God.'

The early Christians can have had no idea of the trouble they were storing up for future Christians when they turned the birth of Jesus into a virgin birth. There can be no doubt that it goes back to the early days of Christianity, but Mark makes no mention of it. If it is true that Mark's Gospel contains the memories of Peter, then that omission is very significant indeed.

In the ancient world there were all sorts of stories of virgin births floating around. The Greek gods were always fathering human children, and you find virgin births in Hinduism as well. As I began to prepare to write about this chapter I read a poem by Robert Frost called *The bearer of Evil Tidings*. It tells an ancient story of a princess en route from China to marry a Persian prince. She was found to be with child 'and though a god was the father' it still seemed better not to continue the journey!

Luke may have thought that he was writing history but many Christians treat the story as simply a beautiful myth.

36–79: The stories continue to the end of the chapter and need no further comment from me except for us to note that John the Baptist and Jesus were related to one another. Mary visits his mother and stays until just before John is born.

Luke has a gift for storytelling and has either written or included two beautiful poems (among the first Christian hymns). So whatever we think of the stories as history, this chapter is a pleasure to read – full of the joy we experience when we are looking forward to the arrival of children.

Chapter Two

1–7: Here Luke is very careful to give his story a firm historical setting. Jesus was born when Quirinius was governor of Syria and when Caesar Augustus decreed 'that all the world should be enrolled.'

How firm is that historical setting? Forgive me for a rather dull examination: Luke may claim to be giving us a historical account but he hasn't done his homework.

> '. . .a decree went out from Caesar Augustus that all the world should be enrolled. This was the first enrolment.

The first enrolment in Judaea caused the revolt against Rome of Judas of Galilee. So far, I haven't been able to discover when that was. Since Gamaliel refers to it shortly after the death of Jesus, it was probably 6 CE (see Acts 5:37). There is no evidence of enrolments in the area before 6 CE. From that date there was a census every fourteen years in Egypt. And there was a census in Syria in 6 CE when Quirinius was legate of Syria and Coponius procurator of Judaea.

Luke claims that the first enrolment was when Quirinius was governor of Syria. Does he mean the census in 6 CE? If so, he is telling us that Jesus was born in 6 CE. But that is long after the death of Herod the Great who features so powerfully in Matthew's story of the birth of Jesus. He died (if I remember rightly) in 4 BCE.

MOST Christian scholars put the birth of Jesus sometime between 6 and 4 BCE. Tertullian put it even further back, between 9 and 6 BCE. This would make Luke's dating quite wrong.

Just to confuse things still further Quirinius MAY HAVE BEEN in Syria from 10–7 BCE and he MAY HAVE BEEN governor of Syria from 3–2 BCE!

2:8–20: I'm sorry to go on about Luke and history but he started it! Twice now he has affirmed his determination towards historical accuracy. He began the Gospel by affirming that that is what he intended to write and he sets this chapter firmly in the days of Caesar Augustus 'when Quirinius was governor of Syria'. Yet his picture of the birth of Jesus is so different from that of Matthew that they can't both be right.

Both Matthew and Luke have Jesus born in Bethlehem. Matthew gives the impression that Bethlehem was Joseph and Mary's home village and that they only moved to Nazareth after the flight to Egypt prompted by Herod's determination to kill their child. By the time they returned Herod was dead but his son

Archelaus was now the ruler and they probably felt that Bethlehem wasn't a safe place to live.

Luke's picture is completely different. He has Joseph and Mary living in Nazareth but required to go to the ancestral home of Joseph's family for the enrolment. (There is no evidence that there was such a requirement. Luke may have misunderstood a later requirement that people who were away from home at the time of the census should go home to enrol.) Luke's story has a journey ending in near disaster with nowhere for the family to stay and the familiar birth in a stable. It is an ideal scene for Christmas nativity stories but it looks very much like fiction. In Matthew's Gospel, Jesus seems to have been born at home – in Bethlehem.

Luke's story continues with shepherds, an angel and – 'a multitude of the heavenly host.' But there are no wise men in Luke, nor any of the rest of Matthew's stories.

Matthew has no shepherds but has the story of the star and the wise men, leading to the flight to Egypt and so on.

Mark has none of these things. He begins with Jesus as an adult. When we reach John's Gospel we shall find that he has none of these things either. So is there ANYTHING that can be relied on in these stories at all?

There are some people who would go so far as to say that the Jesus of the Gospels was never born at all! I'm not one of them. My guess (and it is no more than that) is that Matthew was right in thinking that Bethlehem was Joseph and Mary's home. Jesus was born in their home sometime between 6 and 4 BCE.

For unknown reasons – possibly something to do with Herod and his son Archelaus – they decided to move to Nazareth and that is where Jesus and all his brothers and sisters grew up. Whatever the truth of all that, I think we can rely on the statement in verse 21 that Jesus was circumcised according to Jewish law.

The custom probably had something to do with there being health benefits (apparently there still are) but it has always been something which marked Jews out from others. However, just to muddy the waters a bit – some Protestant Christians also had their children circumcised simply because it was in the Bible as a mark of the chosen people.

2:22–38: Verse 22 is probably a simple statement of fact but are the stories of Simeon and Anna?

Many Christians will have found me far too dismissive of the stories preceding the birth of Jesus. I'm afraid that for me, these stories fall into the same category. They are very beautiful but there is no means of knowing whether there is anything factual in them.

ALL of these stories are clearly designed to inform us that in Jesus we have the birth of someone out of the ordinary and very special. For those who have been brought up on these stories it becomes very difficult to take a cold shower and then simply look at Jesus as we would look at anybody else. But it is only by doing so that we can discover whether there really was anything special about him, and if so, what it was.

Verses 29–32 contain the very beautiful early Christian hymn, the 'Nunc Dimittis'. When the end of life draws near, some of us will pray and others of us will hope that we shall be allowed to depart in peace.

Notice verse 33: Joseph and Mary are referred to as 'his father and mother'. There is no hint that Joseph is anything other than his NATURAL father. I shall refer to this again.

39–40: have Jesus growing up in Nazareth, a good, healthy lad.

2:41–52: These verses contain the ONLY story in the whole of the four Gospels about the childhood of Jesus. When he was 12 years old his parents took him to Jerusalem 'at the feast of the Passover' 'according to custom'.

The story is full of references to Jesus' parents, sometimes together and sometimes singly as his father and his mother. As in verse 33 of this chapter, there is no hint that Joseph was thought of as anything other than the natural father of Jesus.

Is that because the family wanted to keep quiet about the conception of Jesus or is it because Joseph WAS the natural father?

As to the story itself, I can do no better than quote from page 192 of my previous book, *An Unbeliever's Guide to the Bible*:

'When his mother and father went to Jerusalem they were part of a larger group from their village and when it was time to go home, Jesus was left behind in Jerusalem.

'It took his parents THREE DAYS to find him in the Temple. Like any other twelve year old boy, Jesus was surprised at their anxiety and that they were so thick that they didn't know where to look for him. A twelve year old boy? Of course he would be in the temple. Where else?'

And I added that I had heard recently of a little boy whose parents were sunbathing on Weymouth beach. The little boy wandered off as children do and ended up in the kiosk for lost children. Finally his frantic parents found him and he said to them, 'Where have you been?'

They were the ones who were lost, not him.

I remember a vicar's wife commenting on the story of Jesus. 'If I had been his mother I'd have given him a good hiding.' We are not allowed to these days – but I suspect that many of us have a good deal of sympathy with that vicar's wife's point of view.

Chapter Three

1–12: This is the first of Luke's forays into history which can be dated with precision. Tiberius Caesar ruled from 14 to 37 CE and it was in the fifteenth year of that reign that John the Baptist began his ministry.

Other than that, he tells the same story as Mark, enlarges it as Matthew does but with the significant addition of verses 10–14 where we are given a flavour of John's general message. He tells the haves to share their wealth with the have nots. His message to tax collectors needs a bit of explanation.

Tax collectors bought a tax area from the government and were charged with producing a defined sum to the government. Anything they made over and above that sum was theirs to keep! Needless to say, they pushed things as high as they could go. John tells them to play fair. And just as they were charged not to misuse their position so soldiers were charged not to misuse their authority and not to be excessively greedy: 'Be content with your wages.'

I don't know the background to those final words but they are words very familiar today. In fact, this whole message rings out fresh today. The haves are always happy to add to their wealth while telling those who are close to the bottom of the pile to be 'content with their wages' and not to ask for more.

John's message will have been pretty popular with the poor and ignored by the rich until he dared to cross the line and start being pretty blunt about the life-style of Herod the tetrarch and Herodias, his brother's wife. That led to his imprisonment and later, to his death.

The significance of John's prophetic ministry for the New Testament is that it prepared the way for Jesus: 'He who is mightier than I is coming, the thong of whose sandals I am not worthy to untie.'

Jesus was this 'mightier' one, destined to baptise people 'with the Holy Spirit', but first Jesus himself had to be baptised and had to receive the Holy Spirit 'in bodily form, as a dove.'

His baptism was accompanied by a voice from heaven, 'Thou art my beloved Son; with thee I am well pleased.'

All of this gives significant headaches to Christian theologians. Christians claim that Jesus is both really and truly God, one of the three persons of the Godhead, and also that he is really and truly a man just as we are men and women.

The stories of the virgin birth were an attempt to show that Jesus was divine. But now we have a story which shows the Spirit of God entering into the human Jesus (although we should notice that in Matthew's Gospel, John the Baptist thought that this was quite unnecessary, presumably because he felt that Jesus had the Spirit already).

For Christian theologians the questions are: was Jesus always God; or was he only God from this moment; or was he not really God at all, but only a man imbued with the Spirit of God?

It was out of their wrestling with such questions that Christians forged their famous creeds – the church's official line. In the early centuries, those who didn't toe the line were tortured or killed. Nowadays they just argue about these things, and of course, they now belong to separate organisations in uneasy friendship still arguing about the same things.

23–38: Both Matthew and Luke give us genealogies based on the male line, yet they are also the two Gospels which deny that Joseph was really the father of Jesus, so what meaning can these genealogies have?

Nor are the genealogies the same. Is either of them accurate, historical, true?

Luke traces the line back to Adam, the first man, and describes him as another 'son of God', as he would have been if the Bible accounts of creation had been genuine scientific descriptions of the beginnings of things. They weren't, and they weren't intended to be. But just suppose that Luke was right and that there had been an ancestor of Jesus called Adam who was a son of God. Just think of the theological controversies THAT would lead to.

Chapter Four

1–13: **The temptations of Jesus.**

Matthew and Luke have the same temptations in a different order but there is no need for me to comment on them again.

14–30: Luke is the only one to tell us that Jesus began his ministry in his home synagogue at Nazareth. (He was also the only one to tell us that Jesus was about thirty years of age when he began his ministry.) In spite of the lovely message from Isaiah with which he began, and an appreciative response from the congregation, he seems to have gone out of his way to upset them in his main message and he certainly succeeded. They were so angry that they planned to throw him off the hill-top, but there was something about the man and in the end they let him go and 'passing through the midst of them' he went to Capernaum where he began both preaching and healing. Jesus is far from being the only man in history who has had that something about him and so passed through hostile crowds unscathed. One other, who comes to mind, was John Wesley.

31–41: The real beginning of the teaching and healing ministry of Jesus was in Capernaum. Travelling teachers and healers would not have been all that uncommon. In the 1960s, in rural India, they were still to be found moving from village to village. They were, in a way, a part of the village 'entertainment', a break from the ordinary routine at a time when even radio was still a novelty owned by few but shared through amplifiers!

Jesus impressed his hearers. He spoke with 'authority'. Here was no dry as dust academic quoting this, that and the other great scholar from the past and never quite expressing his own opinion. Here was someone who spoke as if he knew what he was talking about and who spoke in a language they all understood, full of stories of hearth and home and rural life.

But he not only spoke. He also healed and his healings seemed miraculous. We are so accustomed to relying on scientific medicine that it is hard for us to think of a time when people relied almost entirely on 'wise women', quacks, and people with 'healing hands'. But we all know of people whose healings have surprised everybody and 'alternative medicine' has become big business.

I am quite sure in my own mind that Jesus WAS a healer and I am just as sure that the extent of his healing ministry has been exaggerated, perhaps even grossly exaggerated. In the stories of his temptation in the wilderness we were told that Jesus eschewed the use of miracles to further his work, yet the Gospels are full of 'miracles'. I'm afraid that I don't give any credence to most of those but Jesus clearly was a compassionate man. Faced with all kinds of physical and psychological ills, he clearly felt that he must do what he could to help. Equally clearly, he sometimes and perhaps often made a real difference. In this chapter we are told that one of the beneficiaries was Simon (Peter)'s mother in law.

But I can't help wondering why he waited until he was about thirty to use gifts he must always have had, or were these part of the gift of the Holy Spirit at his baptism? Was his father dead? Did he have to wait until his brothers were old enough to run the family carpentry business? The questions multiply. Why did Jesus rebuke those who called him 'the Son of God' 'because they knew that he was the Christ'? Surely his ministry was all about letting people know that that was who he was, and persuading them to accept his message and follow him?

The most obvious answer, and so perhaps the right answer, is that it was too early, too dangerous and too divisive for Jesus to acknowledge these titles yet.

But I can't help wondering if there is another answer. If Jesus really was fully human like the rest of us, was he still unsure of himself and what he was about? There's not much sign of it but, in spite of that period in the wilderness, was he still racked with questions about his own ministry? Was he still just that 'son of a carpenter' feeling a bit out of his depth, embarrassed and overwhelmed by people's reactions to him and wondering just what it was that John the Baptist had launched him into – a ministry he had never really fully anticipated?

And was it the praise of other people that changed him to the point where he really did believe that he was the person people said he was?

4:42–44: At this stage of his ministry he was still a very attractive and vulnerable human being. He felt that he had a mission to fulfil and he needed time to himself, space and quiet, an opportunity to recharge his batteries.

Chapter Five

1–11: Luke's account of the 'miraculous' haul of fish needs no miracle. Jesus would have seen the shoal when he was sitting in the boat teaching. The effect on the simple fishermen Simon Peter, James and John does not ring true. Fishermen are not that simple and John's Gospel makes it clear that they have known Jesus ever since the ministry of John the Baptist. Peter was brought to Jesus by his brother Andrew who is not mentioned here.

These fishermen followed Jesus, not because of the shoal of fish but because they had been impressed by him and his teaching. Their discipleship must have had a pretty devastating effect on the family business and perhaps on Peter's wife too.

12–16: The healing of the man with leprosy.

When Luke wrote his Gospel few would have questioned this 'miracle'. Modern man asks whether the man really had leprosy and Christian commentators spend a good deal of time providing their own answers.

The passage shows that Jesus was anxious to demonstrate his faithfulness to the requirements of Jewish religious law and custom.

17–26: This is a lovely story and sometimes I think it would be best just to take it at that level but I'm not going to!

Noticing that Jesus begins with the forgiveness of sins a number of commentators have wondered whether this paralysis was psychosomatic. Even if it was, it is pretty remarkable that Jesus should have recognised the fact.

His question in verse 23, 'Which is easier to say, "Your sins are forgiven you," or to say, "Rise and walk,"?' is unanswerable. Of course, the first is easier to say because no one can test it. Meaningful or meaningless it sounds just the same! But to say 'Rise and walk' and to have the power to make it happen can be tested at once.

Let us also consider the Pharisees' question in verse 21, 'Who can forgive sins but God only?'

The sacrificial system in the Temple was supposed to achieve forgiveness. The right sacrificial offerings made at the right time would do the trick. Were there also people with the authority to proclaim forgiveness on behalf of God as Christian priests claim to do?

Luke clearly intends us to catch the implication that if only God can forgive sins, Jesus must be God, for the healing demonstrates that the man is forgiven.

There is an awful lot about sin in the New Testament (perhaps even more in the Old). The Church seems to spend an excessive amount of time trying to make us feel bad about ourselves: sinful, guilty, unworthy of the goodness of God and therefore in need of salvation.

There ARE times in life when some of us go pretty badly wrong. But when we need forgiveness because we have gone astray we don't need it from a god. We need it from those we have hurt and wronged, although the word 'need' is perhaps too strong even there. We don't have to be forgiven to begin again. We don't even have to forgive ourselves, which is fortunate because we may never be able to forgive ourselves. But we *can* put our misdemeanours behind us. We can rebuild our lives and we can recover a measure of self-respect.

Although there ARE people who can be helped by an authoritative statement telling them that their sins are forgiven; religion, sacrifice, salvation theology are quite irrelevant for most of us. NO ONE, not even a supposedly perfect Jesus, can save anyone else. If we go wrong, we have to find a way to begin again and to do better ourselves. Other people can help but no one can do it for us. In the end it is down to the wrong-doer to make good – and s/he can.

Having said all that, my own impression is that most of this talk about sin, guilt and so on is quite unnecessary. I have spent a lifetime visiting people in their homes and often, telling their life stories. Most people are pretty decent on the whole – warm, friendly and kind. Most of us do our best to live worthwhile lives and to give what we can, if to no one else, at least to our nearest and dearest. We don't pretend to be perfect or to be saints but we live our lives by pretty decent standards and we do our best.

Religion, it seems to me, has got it all wrong. As one faithful member of the Salvation Army said to me recently, 'Why does religion try to make us feel bad all the time?'

27–32: The call of (Matthew) Levi the tax-collector to discipleship was a good excuse for a party. But tax-collectors had a pretty bad reputation and Jesus was criticised for fraternising with them and worse, for eating with them. There has always been a widespread feeling that there is something almost sacramental about eating with people.

In verses 31 and 32 Jesus gives his critics a lovely answer.

97

33–39: Jesus claims to be offering something new compared with the old, tired message of the Pharisees (who were themselves thought of as innovators). And the new teaching Jesus offered was joyful. That element of joy must have been very attractive – some African Christianity seems to have it still.

Chapter Six

1–11: These stories about Sabbath law have a continuing relevance for Christians and strict Sabbatarians, and the story of David invites priests to examine their attitude to the bread and wine of the Eucharist. In fact, we ALL need to be constantly re-examining our priorities in life on a rather larger canvas than the question, 'Is it lawful on the sabbath to do good or to do harm, to save life or to destroy it?'

And those of us who have no 'sabbath' need perhaps to reflect on the importance of time away from work and how best to spend that time.

12–19: **The call of the twelve.**

Jesus chose twelve men to form the nucleus of his following.

Why did he choose such a bunch of nonentities? Most of them were so insignificant that, apart from some pretty far-fetched legends and stories, we know virtually nothing about them.

20–49: **The 'Sermon on the Plain'.**

Here sundry teachings of Jesus have been gathered together. They are all worth examining and many of them are worth following. But I'm sure that they will also raise questions for anyone who reads them carefully and thoughtfully. They certainly raise questions for me.

Luke's version of the Beatitudes is simpler than Matthew's. Matthew's have been deliberately shaped into a more literary and even poetic form. Luke's are also accompanied by a matching set of woes for no particular reason. If these really were (if not precisely the words) part of the teaching of Jesus, they don't reflect on him very well.

Much more attractive and infinitely demanding are his words from verses 27–31. But his charge to 'give to everyone who begs from you' is unwise. A lot of those who beg are 'undeserving poor'. We SHOULD be generous but we should be thoughtful with it so that our generosity really does go to people who will benefit from it.

In verse 35 Jesus claims that 'the Most High. . . is kind to the ungrateful and the selfish.' If that were true then 'the Most High' would be pretty stupid! If people are ungrateful when we are kind and generous there is no point in persisting with kindness. We should find recipients who will show their gratitude by making something of our generosity. And if people are selfish, they deserve nothing.

In verses 37–38 Jesus suggests that we should choose the path of virtue because it leads to rich rewards. This is a constant Biblical refrain. But virtue is only virtue when it is chosen for its own sake without any thought of rewards. But we do need to be reminded that it is right and good not to judge and not to condemn, and it is right and good to forgive.

In verse 40 Jesus claims that 'everyone when he is fully taught will be like his teacher.' But any teacher will tell you that plenty of students soon outstrip their teachers, some of them while they are being taught.

However, if we simply take Jesus at his word, does this mean that his disciples will also become what Christians claim he is – perfect man and perfect God?

Verse 43: those who are troubled as I am by the account of Jesus cursing the fig tree (elsewhere), sometimes take comfort from this verse. They think that perhaps disciples have turned this teaching into a story of something that never happened. I hope they are right, but who knows.

Chapter Seven

1–10: and 11–17: Two remarkable stories and lovely stories too. But if we treat them as factual, then questions arise.

The first is the story of the faith of a centurion in the healing powers of Jesus, and the healing of his servant. How much Jesus actually had to do with the healing, we cannot know. The assumption of the story is that he was responsible for it.

In the second story, Jesus raised a man from death. I choose to doubt it. A significant number of people in ancient Palestine were pronounced dead, then they were buried and then, when it was too late, they came to and failed to escape from their grave. I doubt very much if this young man was really dead but he obviously was ill. Whatever it was, it was fortunate for him and for his mother that Jesus came along at the right time.

18–23: John the Baptist was obviously concerned. The ministry of Jesus was not at all what he had been expecting. Had he picked the wrong man?

We have no means of knowing whether Jesus' answer satisfied him (verses 22–23). It is an idealised picture and a very lovely one but it was limited by Jesus' physical presence and that raises very serious questions.

If Jesus really was God intervening in history, as Christians claim, why is his ministry so limited? Why does one man receive his sight and not another; one lame man walk and not all lame men; one leper receive healing and leprosy not be wiped out – and so on?

If Jesus was doing the things God wanted, why does God not do them universally? Why does he not rid the world of suffering? Indeed, why did he permit suffering in the first place?

Adam and Eve stories and tales of man's sin are no answer to those questions. They only push the questions further back. But these intellectual, 'spiritual' questions are only problems for people who cling to religious faith.

For the rest of us, they do not exist. . .

24–35: Jesus pays tribute to the qualities of John the Baptist and condemns the hypocrisy of those who rejected John and who now reject him, although their prophetic ministries are so completely different.

36–50: Here is another very beautiful story where Jesus appears at his best. I never tire of it.

Chapter Eight

1–3: How is a prophet like Jesus funded?

Here we have the answer. Grateful people (Luke only mentions women) provided for him and for his disciples 'out of their means'.

Sadly there are plenty of con-artists and fraudsters who manage to find funds in the same way.

4–15: The parable of the sower and its interpretation. See also Matthew's Gospel.

16–18: A short, slightly muddled collection of sayings. The more I see of life, politics and governance, the more sure I am of the truth of v. 18: the rich grow richer at the expense of the poor and begrudge the poor the little they have.

19–21: Again and again in the Gospels Jesus shows scant respect for his own family. It is very sad and I find it shameful.

22–25: Recently I read a biography of William Barclay, the famous Bible commentator. Of this passage he said, 'the meaning of the story of Jesus calming the storm is not that Jesus calmed the storm but that wherever Jesus is, the storms of life become a calm.'

Whatever the truth of these stories, that is the way many Christians look at them and it shows why their faith is so valuable to them.

26–39: The healing of the man possessed by demons.

The more I read this story the less I like it. I'm with 'all the people of the surrounding country of the Gerasenes' who 'asked him to depart from them.' (v. 37)

If we take the story as it is told, at the level of their beliefs: Jesus brought about one healing, caused the death of a whole herd of pigs with financial loss for the owner and loss of employment for the herdsman.

Nor does he even show much compassion for the deeply disturbed man he has healed. He offers no ongoing social support, no strengthening companionship, no opportunity to build on his sudden new-found health. Brusquely he dismisses the man, 'Return to your home, and declare how much God has done for you.' (v. 39)

40–56: The healing of Jairus' daughter.

Within the story of the healing of Jairus' daughter is the attractive story of another healing. I only want to comment on Jesus' words, 'I perceive that power has gone forth from me.'

Public service IS demanding and costly. It drains us of both physical and emotional strength and energy. Anyone who has genuinely given of self in the service of others can echo those words of Jesus.

And so to the healing of Jairus' daughter. Christians have always treated this as a raising from death and blithely ignored the clear statement of Jesus in verse 52, so let's put it in capital letters:

'SHE IS NOT DEAD BUT SLEEPING.'

Christians ignore his words to magnify his works.

They still do it and they have always done it. Right from the

101

beginning perfectly ordinary occurrences were blown up out of all proportion and turned into miracles.

Here is a girl who has had some sort of serious fever making everyone desperately anxious for her. By the time Jesus arrives the fever has gone and she is sleeping peacefully. Jesus wakes her and tells the family to give her something to eat.

He didn't even heal her!

All he did was to show a bit of common sense and calm a hysterical family down. Just see what Christians have made of that!

Chapter Nine

1–6: Jesus widens his ministry by sending the 12, preparing them for what they would have to do when he was no longer there.

7–9: The ministry comes to the notice of Herod the tetrarch – a first hint of trouble ahead.

10–17: The feeding of the five thousand. There is no need for me to repeat my comments on this story.

18–27: The core message of Jesus was about 'the kingdom of God'. Now he sets out to show his disciples what it will mean for those who are citizens of that kingdom and he begins by asking, 'Who do people say that I am?' and then, 'Who do you say that I am?'

The people regard him as a prophet but Peter claims that he is 'the Christ of God', or the Jewish Messiah.

Jesus accepts that but goes on to show that the future of 'the Christ of God' is quite unlike anything they would have expected:

> 'The Son of man must suffer many things, and be rejected by the elders and chief priests and scribes, and be killed, and on the third day be raised.' (v. 22)

It is in the light of that, that he lays down the conditions of discipleship: self-denial; taking up the cross daily; surrendering one's life to the service of the kingdom.

Churchill's call to 'blood, sweat and tears' in the Second World War was a bit similar.

Christian discipleship demanded everything the disciple had to offer. The words of this passage are magnificent and very stirring but the promise has yet to be delivered.

28–36: The Transfiguration

Assuming that this experience did take place, was it for the benefit of Jesus or for Peter, John and James?

But did it take place? Over the course of my life-time people have spoken to me of strange, visionary experiences. The nearest I ever came to one was at a time of great personal crisis when, in a dream, every single member of my own family (including one who was dead) came and comforted me.

That experience of my own has led me to believe that when people have these unexplained experiences, there is always a psychological reason for them and if we knew enough, we would understand in full.

For Jesus, the anticipation of all that was to happen to him was clearly such a time of psychological crisis.

37–43: Jesus healed a boy who had epilepsy and whom his disciples had failed to heal.

As a Christian, I found the healings of Jesus and his words about the power of faith and of prayer deeply troubling. Neither I nor my fellow Christians, could heal as Jesus had done and most of our prayers for healing seemed to go unanswered. We felt that we were people of faith. Were we actually part of that 'perverse and faithless generation' Jesus criticised so roundly?

It now seems to me that gifts of healing (outside the realms of scientific medicine) do exist. But they often seem to depend on psychological factors which we still understand very imperfectly. If we don't have gifts of healing, even if we are Christians, that is no cause for dismay, grief or guilt. It is simply a fact of life.

And what of prayer? A hospital chaplain once expressed surprise that most of those for whom he offered to pray asked him not to!

For those who believe in prayer, prayer may be helpful in just the same way that the knowledge that people care about you and are supporting you with their love and their longing for you to get better will also help.

44–45: Jesus' warnings about his own future seem to have fallen consistently on deaf ears.

46–48: A simple corrective to egotism, human pride and ambition.

49–50: 'He that is not against you is for you.'

51–55: Jesus rebuked the fire-brands James and John. I wish that he was always so pacific.

56–62: **The demands of discipleship.**

Sometimes these seem inhuman and just plain wrong. The second man ('Let me go first and bury my father') was actually saying: Let me care for my father until he dies and then I will come and follow you.

It seems altogether wrong to me that Jesus should turn him down and do it so brutally. We all have personal responsibilities to fulfil. Those who care for their elderly and needy relatives deserve our highest respect. But Jesus puts himself and his own demands before all the claims of family love, respect and devotion, including the claims of his own family. I find that shameful.

Chapter Ten

1–16: This is another version of the sending out of the 12 in chapter nine. It contains the charge 'heal the sick' even though we have seen that his disciples lacked healing gifts. And it also includes curses or woes on those who do not welcome the disciples and their message. Such woes do not enhance the ministry of Jesus.

17–24: The disciples return, intoxicated with their success, and Jesus shares their joy. It is the same kind of intoxication an actor feels, lifted by the applause at the final curtain call.

Were the effects just as ephemeral as our joy in going to a fine play or concert? Did their work make any real or significant difference?

Perhaps one or two people had their lives transformed and we shouldn't underestimate the value of that. But society was not changed. The lives of the general population would have been unaffected.

25–28: Jesus tells a lawyer that, to inherit eternal life, all that he needs to do is to keep the two supreme old Jewish laws.

If that is the case, there was no need for his own death on the cross, no need for a new religion, no need, in fact, for any *religion* of any kind. For Jesus it was enough that people love God and love their neighbour.

29–37: The parable of the Good Samaritan.

Here is another of those beautiful stories of Jesus which have both permanent and universal significance.

Jesus intended that we should be influenced by such stories: 'Go and do likewise.'

38–42: My sympathies are with the Marthas of this world, not with the drones who do nothing but sit and talk. My grandmother would have told me that there is plenty of time to sit and talk AFTER the work is done.

Chapter Eleven

1–4: The Lord's Prayer.

Now that religion plays so little part in the life of the average person in England, I am still sometimes asked to include the Lord's Prayer in a ceremony – not prayer in general: just the Lord's Prayer. I often wonder why and what it means to those who ask for it.

Is it a sort of voodoo amulet, a hint of insurance, a hedging of bets, just in case?

How many have any real belief in God the Father or any idea of what they mean when they say, 'thy kingdom come'. How many believe that God will feed them in answer to their prayers.

Of course there IS value in reciting the words about forgiveness and temptation if they remind us of our own need to be forgiving and to try to avoid making wrong or harmful choices in life. But do we think of these things when we say the prayer or do we just rattle off the words by rote?

Until recently, the words of this prayer were a given. That isn't true any more. Youngsters often no longer know the prayer off by heart. The same is true of the famous stories of Jesus, like the Good Samaritan that we have just been talking about.

Late in his teaching career my brother put the story of the Good Samaritan up on the blackboard in Latin and told his class of 5th/6th formers to translate it into English. As soon as they recognised the story they could go home! NO ONE left early!

5–13: This passage contains the famous words of v. 9:

'Ask and it will be given you; seek, and you will find; knock and it will be opened to you.'

In life generally the negative is more true than the positive:

'If you don't ask you won't receive' etc.

But Jesus isn't speaking about life generally. He is speaking quite specifically of the gifts of the Holy Spirit. It is the same message in Matthew's Beatitude, 'Blessed are those who hunger and thirst after righteousness for they shall be satisfied.'

The truth in this passage is that if you want to lead a virtuous and valuable life you do really have to want to. In just the same way, we only give up our addictions to smoking, alcohol, drugs and so on if we really, deeply, determinedly want to.

So this is no light-hearted asking, seeking, knocking. This really is the hunger and thirst of the Beatitude.

14–23: Just as people used to condemn women with knowledge of herbal medicines as witches, so Jesus was condemned as one who used diabolical powers in his healings. Why is it that we find it so difficult just to 'rejoice with those who rejoice'? Wasn't it a good thing that a man recovered his ability to speak?

24–26: In a graphic picture, Jesus warned that cleansing or healing must lead on to new and better things if it is to be effective.

27–32: Having condemned the sour-pusses who dismissed his ministry, Jesus seems to be guilty of similar sour-pussery! The more people praised him, and the more they turned out to listen to him, the more he seemed to condemn them.

33–36: This is another version of Luke 8, 16–17. It demonstrates how the sayings of Jesus were remembered in slightly different ways and then interpreted in slightly different ways too.

37–44: This passage, which looks as if it is about washing hands before meals, is actually about the Pharisees' addiction to ritual observance. It goes on to condemn them for their hunger for social status.

But the use of the hand washing ritual for his lesson is a pity since hand washing *is* something that is important.

45–54: Having condemned the Pharisees, he goes on to condemn lawyers. Such blanket condemnations are never *entirely* just (which is something I try hard to remember when I feel like condemning politicians and bankers today). Nevertheless, there was a good deal of justice in what Jesus said. His condemnations will have made him popular with the crowds but only stored up trouble for him when the finale came.

Chapter Twelve

1–3: Jesus inveighs against hypocrisy and warns against secret vice on the ground that nothing is hidden from God. In today's world, nothing much is hidden from men either.

4–7: This is a little collection of memories of his teaching: he warns people to fear God who 'has power to cast into hell' and then he charges people to have no fears because God cares for each one of them – not one sparrow 'is forgotten before God. Why, even the hairs of your head are all numbered' (which is easier with some of us than with others).

One has to ask whether a God who cares so much could ever cast anyone into hell. Could any of us? We may know some pretty awful people but have any of us ever met anyone worthy of *everlasting* punishment? And what is the point of everlasting punishment anyway?

I wonder whether there are still any of the old hell-fire preachers around. I was lucky enough to grow up in a branch of the church where you never came across them. But I heard recently of a Jesuit priest only forty or so years ago speaking to the boys in his school about fire.

First he painted a picture of fire and its power to burn and destroy and he spoke of the agony of any living thing caught by the fire – thankfully a brief agony before death brought release from pain.

And then he went on to speak of the fires of hell which burn but do not destroy and he spoke of the everlasting agony of those who were being burned but for whom there was no release.

This was his picture of hell. Did he really believe in it? Did he really believe that the God and Father of his Lord Jesus Christ could consign people to this, not because they were bad but just because they didn't believe?

It is no wonder that so few Christians have any real belief in hell but they do find great comfort in the two lovely pictures of God's care. An atheist, with no belief in gods, can still rejoice in a passage which stresses the value both of every human life and

107

also of all other forms of life, forms of life we so often undervalue.

8–12: This passage contains the famous verse (10) 'he who blasphemes against the Holy Spirit will not be forgiven.'

A good deal of ink has been used to try to work out what this means. To an atheist it has no meaning at all There are plenty of crimes which many of us call 'unforgivable' but that is not at all what Jesus is on about. If there are no gods there is no such thing as blasphemy.

Jesus also talks about judgement after death and he clearly felt that he would have a say in such judgements. If you don't believe in life after death, passages like this have no meaning for you.

But verses 11 and 12 DO have their value when they warn us against anxiety in the face of injustice. We may not believe in the Holy Spirit but it is simple fact that if we are anxious and troubled we shall not do ourselves justice. If we can keep calm we shall be able to cope with most situations and express ourselves and our own point of view clearly and with the convincing power of simple truth.

13–31: Ours is an age which has become very focussed on material possession and it is the constant purpose of advertising to keep our focus there. We are no longer happy to use hand-me-downs from our parents or grandparents (unless those hand-me-downs are valuable antiques!). We are obsessed with things that are new and with the need to keep updating things we have, even before we have had decent wear out of the old. Things are even made today with obsolescence built into them. This gives relevance to the words: 'Beware of all covetousness; for a man's life does not consist in the abundance of his possessions.' (v. 15)

This verse and the story which follows warn us of the uncertainty of life. It follows that we should make the most both of our lives and of our possessions in the present.

Today's covetousness has led to the kind of sheer unadulterated greed which marks so much of the life of our top bankers and businessmen. NO ONE is worth the kind of money they pay themselves.

But there is always another side to the coin. Jesus tells us to 'take no thought for the morrow' but we must! Simple prudence requires us to recognise that most of us are living longer and that therefore we must provide for the time when we can no longer work and when the state pension will be inadequate. So the message of verses 22–31 is thoroughly wrong-headed. Jesus should have remembered both the dream and the wisdom of Joseph in the later chapters of Genesis.

Willy nilly, most of us HAVE TO spend a great deal of our time thinking about how we can earn enough to pay the bills.

Nor is Jesus right about the birds. They work very hard to find food, create homes and feed their young. And 'God' does not always look out for them. In times of extreme weather it isn't just humans who suffer: the birds of the air, the lilies of the field and even the humble grass can all suffer and die.

But there ARE things in this passage which still have relevance. Our age is one which concerns itself far too much with outward appearances: shape, physical beauty and so on. I suspect that Jesus would have had a good deal to say about much plastic surgery and the cosmetics industry for example.

Without being too much of a puritan it is right to ask the question where true beauty lies. Plastic surgery and make-up can never make up for impurities or deficiencies of character. LASTING beauty does not lie in outward appearance, size or shape. It is in character of real quality that true beauty lies.

32–34: By following these directions literally, the early church in Jerusalem soon put itself and its congregation into a real financial mess so that it had to be bailed out by Gentile Christians from far and wide. If this really was the teaching of Jesus, then he was either thoroughly irresponsible or utterly clueless. But that does not alter the fundamental truth of the words:

'Where your treasure is, there will your heart be also.'

These words invite us to ask where our own treasure lies, in material possessions or in the people we love?

35–48: Jesus speaks of masters and servants without ever calling in question a society which allows some to be masters and some to be servants. And we still haven't learned. Privileged birth, power and wealth, still allow the few to laud it over the many and to treat their fellow human beings as of little account.

In all of this, Jesus regards himself as a master who will go away and return 'at an hour you do not expect.' He should remember his own words 'call no man master'. But in the second half of verse 48 he does get things right:

'Every one to whom much is given, of him will much be required; and of him to whom men commit much they will demand the more.'

49–53: These words have proved to be terribly true. If Christians had really taken them to heart would they have been so ready to follow Jesus? Do we really want a leader who has come to give division, a man who divides families and sets them against one another? Or do we seek leaders who strive 'to give peace on earth'?

It is a plain, simple, tragic and terrible fact that from the very beginning Jesus has proved to be divisive. His followers have split from their kith and kin and then from one another, killing and torturing one another in his name. This has been the story of Christianity throughout history.

54–56: These are strange verses. Why condemn us as hypocrites for trying to understand the world we live in? That attempt to understand has brought us so much that is good.

Of course, Jesus is talking about something else when he says that we 'do not know how to interpret the present time'. On his terms, we never did and we never will. It is surely better to go on quietly studying the facts and learning what their implications are for human life.

57–59: This is simply a piece of good advice – all the more valuable now that we seem to be following the American predilection for running to litigation at the slightest provocation.

Chapter Thirteen

1–5: The question is, 'Do we suffer in life because we are sinful?'

The answer to the two examples given is 'No.' With different examples it might just as well have been 'yes'!

The first example seems to have been punishment for rebellion (raised perhaps by yet another man who claimed to be the Messiah). The second example is of an accident.

People often do ask irrational questions after accidents even when the actual causes of death are obvious. The question is often 'why me' or 'why him, or her, or them' as if we are being punished for some unknown misdemeanour. It is a baffling response. Accidents are often due to folly or carelessness or just bad judgement. And they are sometimes due to bad workmanship. But sin is the wrong word to use, implying as it does, divine judgement.

Incidentally, I read recently that the New Testament uses five different words for sin whereas it only uses three for love. I wonder what that tells us – if it tells us anything at all!

On this occasion Jesus used the question to call people to repent because 'unless you repent you will all likewise perish.' (v. 5)

In point of fact, with or without repentance, all of us will perish sooner or later. That is our human destiny so there is no point in worrying about it or making a big thing of it. As long as it doesn't come before it is due it is simply something to be accepted and faced when our time comes.

6–9: This parable shows the vinedresser demonstrating a much more caring attitude to his fig tree than the attitude Jesus showed when he cursed a fig tree.

10–17: A lovely story about a healing, sour grapes and kindness, decency and common sense from Jesus.

18–21: Sayings of Jesus about the kingdom of God and its unseen growth.

22–30: Jesus speaks of all those who will be included and all those who will be excluded from the kingdom of God.

I don't feel the need to comment on any of these things.

31–35: Warned that 'Herod wants to kill you', Jesus speaks of the path he must follow, a path over which Herod has no control.

His lament over Jerusalem is very moving. I wonder what he would think of Jerusalem, that symbol of religious and national discord, now?

Chapter Fourteen

1–6: As we have seen, one of the criticisms of Jesus was that he broke the rules and regulations governing the Sabbath, the Jewish holy day. His answers to his critics were unanswerable. There are some things which always take priority over our petty rules and regulations.

7–11: Jesus had no time for petty place-seekers:

'For everyone who exalts himself will be humbled, and he who humbles himself will be exalted.'

Unfortunately that isn't always true!

12–14: But for the last sentence this is a perfect illustration of charitable giving. Jesus spoils it with his promise of a final reward. Giving is its own reward. It needs nothing more.

15–24: This is a story well worth pondering. You can't help wondering why all those invited cried off. But it is good that the banquet, far from being wasted, was enjoyed by people who really benefitted from it.

As one who has now turned down the invitation to Jesus' banquet, I hope that those who still enjoy it really benefit from it. But are they really prepared for the demands Jesus makes in verses 25–33.

25–33: Sometimes people claim that Jesus is using extreme language for effect and that we are not to take him literally. It is a kind attempt to soften his demands, but those demands were made so often that I don't think they can be watered down.

A man must have a pretty high opinion of himself to make such demands – and all sorts of people have made them. None of us can dictate to our neighbour what his response should be, but it seems to me that our human lives are so precious that they should not be surrendered to anybody else or to any particular dogma.

We have but one life to live and it is one of the few things we can ever really call our own. How we live that life is up to us. No one else has the right to claim that life for themselves.

34–35: Perhaps Jesus has not fully realised that it is often when people surrender their own lives and cease to choose their own path that they lose their savour and become dull – less than they once were. Every parody of marriage expresses that truth.

Chapter Fifteen

1–2: Jesus was criticised for the company he kept.

Sometimes it is right to be concerned at the company people keep. Bad company can easily lead us astray. But in the case of Jesus the criticism was unjust. His sole aim was to lift people into a better life.

3–32: I have been looking forward to reading the three parables of chapter 15 again. They are among the loveliest Jesus ever told. I've no idea whether he added the moral himself or whether Luke did that for him. Many of the children's stories of my childhood had a moral attached. It often didn't seem to belong

112

(even to me as a child) and it usually seemed a pity, taking the edge off the story.

The moral we are given for these stories is that 'there will be more joy in heaven over one sinner who repents than over ninety-nine righteous persons who need no repentance.' (v. 7)

That's fair enough. There always is great joy when someone whose life is in a mess for one reason or another, gets it together and manages to start again. But I prefer to let the stories make their own impact without pointing morals. That seems to me to be the way the best storytellers have always operated, which makes me wonder whether Jesus just told his stories and left it at that. These three are of lasting value and universal relevance and show why it is that Jesus is still appreciated as a fine moral teacher.

The first is the well-known parable of the lost sheep. The second is less well-known and at first sight might seem a bit trivial. Why would a woman bother so much over such an insignificant coin as a drachma – the sort of coin that falls out of your trouser-pocket and gets lost under the sofa cushions?

It has been suggested that the coin was probably from her wedding head-dress so its loss was almost equivalent to the loss of a wedding ring. The recovery of a lost wedding ring really would be cause for rejoicing.

The third story from verse 11 onwards is the famous story of the prodigal son. Every part of it rings true.

Chapter Sixteen

1–9: This is a thoroughly baffling story. Jesus seems to be commending dishonesty and sharp practice. He isn't. He is only commending prudence but he could surely have found a better way of doing so!

10–17: Here are some collected sayings, which begin by correcting the impression given in verses 1–9. But when Jesus says that no man can serve two masters he is wrong. Many of us have to if we are to make ends meet.

18: This verse about marriage has given Christians endless trouble. British society has gone its own way and ignored what Jesus said completely. The Christian church can never make up its mind whether to stick to the teaching of Jesus or to follow the lead of society and accept or even approve what people actually do. Matthew's Gospel already shows the church trying to soften down the words of Jesus a bit. The teaching and practice of the church on marriage nowadays is a confused and sometimes hypocritical mess.

19–31: **The rich man and Lazarus.**

Does the unbelievable story of the resurrection of Lazarus, the brother of Martha and Mary, spring from this story I wonder?

Even this story of justice, reward and punishment is no more than a pipe-dream, unless there really is life after death. I don't believe that there is, so for me, there is no bliss for the beggars of this world and no judgement on the heedless rich. It is that which makes excessive wealth so thoroughly obnoxious and hateful.

Chapter Seventeen

1–4: Jesus pronounces a pretty devastating woe on those who lead others astray. Most of us would approve his sentiments. But a woe doesn't actually do anything or achieve anything other than relieve our feelings.

Jesus is more useful when he speaks of honesty, repentance and forgiveness. When we go wrong the ideal person to tell us so is ourselves. It is when we know in ourselves that we have gone wrong that we are most likely to change.

Failing that, we do need someone who is a close enough friend to be able to be honest with us without destroying our friendship. And if we manage to change and put our wrong-doing behind us, we also need people to welcome that and to help us in the new start we are making – and that really is what forgiveness is all about.

5–6: Overblown and extravagant statements like this do not help the cause of a faith, especially when naive people think that they have to take them literally.

7–10: Jesus doesn't seem to have a very high opinion of the master/servant relationship yet he never questions it.

Any master who behaved like this one would deserve bad and surly servants. But it is high time that we recognised that ANY kind of master/servant relationship is wrong. None of us is more than a human being and none of us is less.

11–19: Here is a story which expresses a sad fact of life. Only one in ten of those healed returned to Jesus to thank him. At my school, when I was a boy, there was a middle-aged lady who worked in the kitchens and had been a good friend to generations of schoolboys. When she retired, I wrote to her. It seemed only right. She had shown us a great deal of kindness. Apparently I was the only boy to write.

One of the finest contributions the Methodist Church has made to Christian worship is the annual Covenant Service. As with most written services, it has changed over time and it seems no longer to contain a phrase which haunted me as a young man and lives with me still – or rather, almost lives, for I was never any good at remembering things properly:

'We have received great benefits with little thanks.'

The words 'thank you' are so inadequate but the expression of gratitude is so important.

20–27: Jesus tells, first the Pharisees, and then the disciples, that the kingdom of God will come without warning. He suggests that its coming will be as awful as Noah's flood and as the destruction of Sodom and Gomorrah, or as modern natural disasters which have caused so much loss, distress and devastation. Therefore his disciples must always be ready for the coming of the kingdom.

Jesus seems to have no problem with mass slaughter and devastation just so long as the Noah's and Lot's of this world are saved from it all. It's a bleak arid inhuman message – but his disciples have been waiting so long that most of them don't really believe it any more.

The final, memorable sentence is, of course, true:

'Where the body is, there the eagles will be gathered together.'

Chapter Eighteen

1–8: Here is another odd story encouraging people to 'pray and not lose heart'. The implication is that God has to be pressured into doing what is right. That is not what Jesus meant but it is what it sounds like. Since he actually believed that God would vindicate those who pray 'speedily', he chose an odd illustration and not a very suitable one.

Although I no longer believe in prayer, I do recognise the value of regular times of quiet for reflection, meditation and so on.

9–14: Here is a brilliant portrayal of self-righteousness ('I

115

thank thee that I am not like other men') and self-abasement, ending with a message we have heard before, one which does not necessarily apply in real life.

15–17: This is a much-loved picture of Jesus with children and of his approval of childlike innocence in his followers.

18–30: Here is another story about the cost of discipleship. Jesus sees that a man is too attached to his wealth and demands that he get rid of it all, it doesn't follow that he would make the same demand of EVERY wealthy man or woman. But perhaps, since this man was clearly someone decent and virtuous, if he had thought about it more carefully, he could have found a more acceptable path of discipleship rather than just sending him away feeling miserable and despondent.

When the man had gone he praised those who had put him and his kingdom before 'wife or brothers' (never mind sisters!) 'or parents or children' and promises great rewards. His praise raises a number of questions.

Were people/are people right to put Jesus before every natural intimate human relationship and was Jesus right to praise them in this way?

If they were, or are, right to put Jesus first, should Jesus have offered them rewards? Should they not have chosen to follow him without any thought of reward?

And last but not least, was there any real meaning in the rewards Jesus offered?

My own answers to those questions are probably pretty obvious but it is not for me to answer for other people.

31–34: Jesus probably did try to prepare his disciples for all that would happen in Jerusalem but since he could not know precisely what would happen, he probably didn't give these specific details. They are provided after the event.

Nothing in the ministry so far will have prepared them for these things. Nor has there been anything to show why Jesus would seek such confrontation or why the authorities should feel that they had to take such extreme measures.

It is true that he wasn't very polite to them but most of us are just as rude about our own political leaders and the people at the top of our society.

It is also true that he broke many of their rules and regulations but these were of little more significance (yes, a little more, given that they were religious) than most speeding offences today.

Everything points to the possibility that he could have gone on wandering about the country preaching his message, telling his stories and healing the sick and no one would have done more than criticise him. So why did he actively seek such confrontation?

With hindsight we can see that if he had simply continued with his ministry indefinitely, no one would remember him now except in the way we remember other ancient teachers. It was his death in Jerusalem and the belief of his disciples that he had risen to life again that put him on the world stage. Did he really foresee all that? We must think of these things more carefully in due course. For now it is enough that 'his disciples understood none of these things.' (v. 34)

35–43: The healing of a blind man – almost as if Luke is agreeing with me and saying, 'Now this is what he ought to be doing'!

Chapter Nineteen

1–10: The transformation of a rich tax-collector into an honest benefactor. Notice that Jesus does not ask Zacchaeus to give up all *his* wealth.

If the healing of the blind man at the end of chapter eighteen and the transformation of Zacchaeus really happened, these were wonderfully worthwhile things Jesus could have gone on doing indefinitely. Instead, he chose the path of confrontation which led to his death.

6–27: The parable of the talents.

This is a fairly stark parable. Parables, like other illustrations, should not be expected to endure too close scrutiny. They make their point and are not intended to do more than that.

Nevertheless, the third servant hardly deserved to be called 'wicked'. He was honest, worried, timid and fearful. It was the nobleman who was at fault. He should have known this man better and recognised that he was not cut out to be a businessman.

That doesn't alter the value of the basic message of this parable that each of us should make use of whatever talents we have and, as we use them, our range of ability will broaden, deepen and increase.

In the parable the two who used the talents did so for the benefit of the nobleman and of themselves. In real life it is important that we should use our talents, not just for ourselves but for the benefit of the community at large.

28–40: We have already read this story and noted that Jesus had clearly made his preparations for his entry into Jerusalem.

41–44: The entry into Jerusalem caused plenty of excitement amongst the disciples but Jesus didn't share it. He wept over Jerusalem, foreseeing its destruction. If he saw it today would he still weep over it and cry, 'Would that even today you knew the things that make for peace'?

There are many of us in many parts of the world faced with the folly of our political leaders, who must have felt time and again the same kind of grief and the same helpless despair. Would that even today men knew the things that make for peace.

45–46: Luke disposes of the cleansing of the temple in two verses.

47–48: He was teaching daily in the temple. Notice that no one stopped him. There is still no clear reason why 'the chief priests and the scribes and the principal men of the people sought to destroy him.'

As far as we can see he was no more than a nuisance to them. They would want to undermine him and to get him out of the city but surely not more. The story as it is told still just doesn't add up.

Chapter Twenty

1–8: In argument, Jesus was extremely quick-witted and more than a match for the Jewish authorities. Added to that, the crowds of visiting pilgrims from outside Jerusalem were on his side.

But I find myself asking all sorts of questions I have never asked before. They asked Jesus the source of his authority. Since they WERE the authorities in Jerusalem, why didn't they simply find a quiet moment to arrest him, keep him in prison until the festival was over, and then simply send him out of the city? It would have been easy enough for them to do.

9–18: I have also been trying to puzzle out why on earth they bothered to kill him. Much of his teaching had been acceptable to them and the rest, no more than a mild irritant. His healings –

118

even those on the Sabbath – gave the authorities no reason to kill him. So why did they?

Did the message of Jesus become more extreme and strident in Jerusalem? Did his claims for himself become more specific and extreme?

The parable in verses 9–18 speaks of the way the Jews had always rejected the message of their prophets. Jesus claims to be, not just one in the line of prophets, but the son of God.

Here, for the first time, there is a claim which would seem to the priests to be blasphemous and deserving of death.

It is difficult for those of us who are not religious to see why religious people take blasphemy so seriously but they do. Jesus himself did. To the Jews it was deserving of death (although, as we shall see, not to the Romans).

19–26: Once again, Jesus shows himself more than a match for trick questions.

27–40: The Sadducees (who were priests) asked a trick question about the resurrection. Belief in resurrection was comparatively new amongst the Jews. It was by no means universal and the Sadducees did not hold with it.

But Jesus (and the Pharisees) did believe in resurrection to a life where people became 'equal to angels and are sons' (and presumably daughters) 'of God.' God is 'not God of the dead, but of the living.'

In the nature of things, belief in resurrection or in any kind of life after death, is a matter of faith. We cannot KNOW one way or the other. Those who believe in resurrection have as much right to their belief as those who do not. But at the very least it seems sensible to me to base our lives on the things we know rather than on the things we hope or believe.

41–44: Jesus is at pains to point out that he is Lord of the ancient king David, so it seems strange that both Matthew and Luke have taken such pains to establish Jesus as being of the line of David (in fulfilment of Old Testament prophecy).

Have they missed the implications of this claim? Jesus suggests here that before his earthly life he was always Lord. So he speaks of his pre-human existence as well as of his resurrection to post-human existence. John's Gospel will make these claims much more explicit.

If the priests were aware of these claims, once again they

would have felt that they were utterly blasphemous and worthy of death.

45–47: Although this condemnation of the scribes was no doubt true of many of them, it wouldn't exactly have endeared him to them, and I can't believe it was true of them all.

Chapter Twenty-one

1–4: I have already commented on the widow's gifts.

5–38: This is a vivid picture of human life as it is, as it has always been and sadly, as it always will be unless we learn to live in peace with one another – and even then, natural disasters are inescapable.

Within this picture, there are other pictures:

There is a picture of the persecution of Christians, but not the rather worse picture of the persecution of Christians by other Christians or the persecution of all sorts of other people by Christians. These things were not foreseen but have been utterly shameful.

There is also a picture of the fall of Jerusalem which took place twice in just over a century. There is no vision of the long term future of the city or the follies and horrors it has inspired.

Finally there is a picture of the second coming of Jesus 'in a cloud with power and great glory'. 2000 years on that remains something for the future. That rather undermines Jesus' claim in verses 29–33 that 'this generation will not pass away till all has taken place.'

If these words really were his words, then he got it wrong. How much more did he get wrong? It is hard for present day disciples to take seriously his warning that they should live their lives in constant readiness. But that doesn't alter the fact that all of us, regardless of our religion or irreligion, should always seek to live our lives so that they can come out of the closest scrutiny with honour.

Chapter Twenty-two:

1–2: Here another reason is given for the authorities' determination to put Jesus to death: he was too popular. They clearly feared public disturbance which would have brought the Romans down on them like a ton of bricks.

Native authorities in countries ruled as part of an empire have to be very careful to keep dissident sections of their population under control if they are to keep their own privileges and authority.

3–6: Luke adds nothing to our picture of Judas.

7–13: Just as Jesus had made prior preparations for his triumphal entry into Jerusalem, so he has made private preparations to keep the Jewish Passover – the Jewish celebration of their release from slavery in Egypt many centuries earlier. We need not trouble ourselves about scholarly doubts as to whether it really was the Passover that Jesus celebrated.

14–34: As we have seen, the words of Jesus during the Last Supper have become the foundation of the central Christian act of worship.

At these supremely important moments of the story we are side-tracked by talk of betrayal and by arguments over who is the greatest of the disciples. It is all rather pathetic. Here at the very end of his ministry he finds that his closest followers have learned nothing.

He singles out Simon Peter as one who will let him down and then recover even though they will all do so. 'I have prayed for you that your faith may not fail.' (v. 32)

Had he also prayed for Judas? If not, why not?

And if so, why has his prayer not been successful?

35–38: This obscure passage makes it clear that in the future the disciples must be ready for anything, but the advice to buy swords seems very strange.

39–46: The whole chapter has shown Jesus to be severely stressed and that reaches its height as he prays in the Garden of Gethsemane. But this time of prayer also brings him a composure which never deserts him. Whatever we think about this last period of his life, he achieved a dignity and composure which few men could have sustained.

His disciples were completely out of their depth, lost and exhausted, which suggests that the previous days in Jerusalem must have been much more demanding than the Gospels reveal.

47–53: From the agony of Jesus and his achievement of dignified composure we move to the bathos of his betrayal and the sword cutting off a servant's ear! Even Shakespeare could not

f

have switched more completely from the depths of human tragedy and emotion to pure farce.

54–62: And so we come to the moving account of Peter's weakness, failure and distress. It is one of the most touching stories in the Gospels. I have always felt for Peter, and with him too, for here is a man of genuine humanity. He comes across as one of the most genuinely and warmly human of all the disciples and happily, he was to recover from these moments to become one of the supreme leaders of the infant Christian Church – although he was never quite all that the Roman Catholic church claims for him.

63–65: Here we see man's petty inhumanity, the sort of thing that has always been, and is still, desperately common wherever pathetic, small minded people are given a little bit of authority and power.

Today it surfaces in the army, in police forces, in prisons and sometimes even in nursing homes. It is one of the sadder and nastier facts of life. When political and religious leaders connive at it, brush it under the carpet, or are even just silent about it, they are themselves tainted and we all share their taint.

66–73: Here the authorities were concerned to establish just what it was that Jesus was claiming for himself and who he claimed to be. Did he claim to be 'the Christ', the Jewish Messiah? That would not have come as any great surprise. There were many who made the same claim.

But when it became clear that he actually claimed to be in some unique sense 'the Son of God', then in their eyes it was clear that he was guilty of blasphemy and therefore deserving of death.

Jesus clearly did believe that he was what he claimed to be. Nobody, other than Christians, has ever accepted those claims. Jews do not. Moslems, who treat Jesus with considerable respect, do not.

The rest of us can respect and welcome a good deal of his teaching and many of the things he did, but that is all. The society in which he lived was dominated by its religion, but it was also a bit of a political hot-house, like a cauldron always bubbling over. Jesus was a man of that society. There is so much that is good and admirable about him, but in the end he claimed too much for himself, perhaps led astray by the adulation he received.

So the authorities condemned him to death for blasphemy. But they didn't actually have the authority to put him to death. That was the prerogative reserved by the Roman authorities and the Romans (who were not religious in the Jewish sense) didn't put people to death for blasphemy. An alternative charge had to be brought. It was found in the central teaching of Jesus about the kingdom of God He was charged with claiming to be 'the king of the Jews.'

That was something which the Romans WOULD take seriously.

Chapter Twenty-three

1–5: The Roman Governor, Pilate, was not convinced and didn't really want to get involved in what he saw as internal Jewish squabbles. Learning that Jesus was a Galilean he tried to pass the buck and sent Jesus to Herod Antipas who ruled Galilee for the Romans.

Herod's questions elicited no reply from Jesus just as Pilate's had failed to do. Jesus chose a dignified silence. It must have looked to his accusers very much like a claim to superiority. Jesus must have seemed to be saying, 'I am above all this pettiness', which will not have endeared him to his accusers.

Luke claims that if nothing else was achieved, the case brought a new harmony into the personal relationship between Pilate and Herod! Herod sent Jesus back to Pilate.

13–25: The proper judgement of the court was very simple:

'I did not find this man guilty of any of your charges against him; neither did Herod. . . nothing deserving death has been done by him; I will therefore chastise him and release him.' (vvs. 14b–17)

Even the chastisement was a sop to them. And that should have been the end of the matter. But those who have watched our own governments faced with so-called 'terrorists' will recognise that the judgements of the court rarely are the end of the matter.

On this occasion, two things played into the hands of the Jewish authorities. One was their control of the mob.

We may wonder how crowds which had cheered Jesus so enthusiastically when he rode into Jerusalem one week could be shouting for his death a week later. Crowds ARE notoriously fickle, but the real answer is that they were different crowds, comprised of different people.

Jesus' following came from outside Jerusalem. The cheering crowds of pilgrims on their way to Jerusalem for the festival knew him; knew of his ministry; and anyway, were happy people ready to cheer anyone for any reason.

Within Jerusalem it was a different story. Jesus was hardly known and the crowds were in the control of the Temple authorities. Think perhaps of a Scot or a Cornishman, popular in his own area of the Highlands or the far west, but unknown in London. He wouldn't stand a chance.

The other thing that played into the hands of the Jewish authorities was the custom pinpointed in Matthew and Mark, the custom of releasing a criminal at Passover time. The crowd had been primed to demand the release of Barabbas rather than Jesus and Pilate gave way to mob pressure. So a man who had done 'nothing deserving death' was 'delivered up to their will.' (vvs. 15 & 35)

26–38: So Jesus was crucified.

The story is simply told. Physically weakened, Jesus needed the help of a conscript, Simon of Cyrene, to carry the cross. Did he really flare up with one final warning about the fate of Jerusalem, like a flame from a dying ember?

He was crucified with two criminals but distinguished by the inscription showing why the Romans were prepared to let him die. Mocked and scorned, he preserved his dignity. Luke preserves three things Jesus said on the cross. The first was for all those responsible for his death:

'Father, forgive them; for they know not what they do.' (v. 34)

The second was to one of the criminals dying with him, a man impressed by his dignity and innocence:

'Today you will be with me in Paradise.' (v. 43)

And finally, immediately before his death:

'Father, into your hands I commit my spirit!' (v. 46)

The Roman centurion in charge of the crucifixion was also impressed:

'Certainly this man was innocent.' (v. 47)

Christian mythologising has added to those words. It is to Luke's credit that he didn't. Indeed, Luke's whole story of the crucifixion is marked by its simplicity and we are the more impressed by Jesus because of it.

He gives us a straightforward account of the tragic and unnecessary death of an innocent man. That is all. There is NOTHING here to suggest the huge edifice of Christian sacrificial theology which has been built upon the death of Jesus.

50–56: Joseph of Arimathea 'a good and righteous man, who had not consented to their purpose and deed' (vvs. 50–51) saw to the burial of Jesus and some of the female disciples saw where Jesus was buried.

Chapter Twenty-four

1–11: Luke tells the story of the empty tomb and the message to the women that Jesus had risen from the dead. The story is basically the same as that in Matthew and Mark but there are differences in detail.

13–35: Luke has a story about the resurrection which is not found elsewhere. It is a lovely story but it raises all sorts of questions, even for people who believe in the resurrection.

Why would Jesus choose to reveal himself to two disciples who are completely unknown, one of whom isn't even named?

Notice that already the simple story of the empty tomb is beginning to grow. Luke said that the women saw two men at the tomb. They have now become a 'vision of angels.' (v. 23)

In this story, Jesus explained everything that had happened to these two unknown disciples. They didn't recognise him until the three of them sat at table and broke bread together. The imagery is that of the Last Supper but, unless the unnamed disciple was one of the twelve, these two disciples were not present at the Last Supper.

The story doesn't bear too close examination but it is a lovely story, and for those of us who are not Christian it should perhaps be viewed simply in that light.

36–43: Here are 'proofs' that the risen Jesus has achieved a physical resurrection. Many *Christians* find these 'proofs' unconvincing, let alone the rest of us. They raise all sorts of additional questions about the nature of the body of the risen

Christ. They even raise the question of whether Jesus actually did die upon the cross. Was he revived in the coolness of the tomb?

Even though, as I have mentioned elsewhere, people were sometimes buried while they were still alive (by mistake, I hasten to add!), that is a speculation which never cut much ice with me – until last week.

So let's have a rest from all of this seriousness for a while.

A week ago I woke in the middle of the night with what felt like a cannonball in my stomach. I spent the night retching and being sick and then I spent the whole of the following day asleep eating nothing. I would have been quite happy to die.

The next day I woke feeling fragile but much better and that lasted until teatime when I was pretty groggy again.

Then came a day when I had to go to work and my wife was so worried about me that she drove the car. Throughout this period I had virtually nothing to eat. And then, apart from continuing weakness, it was all over.

Could Jesus have been buried alive, slept in the tomb, woken, weak and fragile, and been released? There are some who think so. I don't. Those who do, still have to explain what happened next to this man recovered from his wounds.

There is so much speculation but none of it leads anywhere.

44–49: Here at least we are on fairly solid ground. Verses 46–49 spell it all out and show us the purpose behind the confrontation, the death and the resurrection of Jesus.

First, it was the fulfilment of the Old Testament prophets. That is one of the consistent claims of the early church. Attempts to show this to be literally true require a considerable stretching of the meaning of Old Testament passages. But in general terms the claim is fair. Jesus built upon the teaching of the Old Testament prophets, took the best of it, moved it forward and made it more human.

Secondly, the fulfilment of the Old Testament included the sufferings and resurrection. Except for the fact that some of the prophets did suffer, that seems to me to stretch the Old Testament beyond credibility.

Third, the purpose of it all was that 'repentance and forgiveness of sins' should no longer be limited to the Jews but 'should be preached in the name of Jesus to all nations.'

126

That purpose has been fulfilled and I want to comment on that more fully in a moment or two. But I cannot, for the life of me, see that that purpose required the death or the resurrection of Jesus. His call to repentance and his message of forgiveness could have gone round the world without the crucifixion.

Finally, the fulfilment of the purpose of the life and ministry of Jesus must wait upon 'the promise of my Father', 'power from on high' – in other words, the gift of the Holy Spirit which was to become the beginning of the story of Luke's sequel to his Gospel, 'the Acts of the Apostles', a book which shows the beginnings of the fulfilment of the purpose of Jesus.

50–52: The sightings of the risen Jesus are over. The ministry of Jesus is over. The purpose of it all has been revealed. With one final blessing, and grieving disciples now full of joy, the story ends.

It is an impressive finale expressed beautifully and with simple clarity. Luke has answered my questions to his own satisfaction if not to mine. He has shown Jesus as a man who had a driving purpose which led him and enabled him to face death itself – and in Luke's view, to triumph over death by resurrection.

The result of all this is that the purpose of Jesus has been pretty comprehensively fulfilled and is still being fulfilled. The Gospel of Jesus has been preached to all nations and, whatever else it has been, it has been a Gospel of repentance and forgiveness of sins. In the process, Christianity has become one of the greatest of all world religions. This is one of the supreme human achievements of all time and it cannot just be brushed to one side.

As I look at the massive achievements that have followed from the life and work of Jesus it seems to me that two things have happened. The first of them is tragic.

Christians have taken the Jewish religion as it was in Jerusalem, based on the Temple and the sacrificial worship of the Temple and they have simply transformed it into a world-wide institution. That institution centres on glorious and expensive churches built by people whose pay was minimal and who lived their own lives in poverty and squalor. Although those churches do not sacrifice lambs or doves, their worship does focus on 'the sacrifice of the Mass' and on a sacrificial theology which seems far removed from the teaching of Jesus.

Within that church, without having to try very hard, you can find everything that appalled Jesus; everything against which he stood; everything in religion he hated and condemned. All the things he denounced in Jerusalem are now to be found on a universal stage and it has all been done in his name. That is the terrible tragedy and irony of the growth of the Church.

Fortunately the story is not all tragedy. Within that flawed institution the fundamental teachings of Jesus can still be found. Both because of the church and in spite of the church, those teachings have been shared with people throughout the world and they have achieved and continue to achieve a great deal that is good. They have been the inspiration for some of the best things humans have ever done for one another. And they have helped masses of people to live good, decent, even noble lives. Throughout the world there are ordinary, straightforward followers of Jesus of Nazareth whose piety and goodness deserve his title 'the salt of the earth'. He would have loved them.

There are many more like them who are nothing to do with the Christian church and may never have heard the name of Jesus or listened to his message. These too, the ordinary, decent people of all religions and none, who get on with their lives without fuss and do their best for one another and for the world in which they live, are worthy of that title.

Christian or non-Christian, religious or not religious, these are the people on whom every society really depends and for whom we should reserve our highest praise. It is the love, kindness, decency, forgiveness and friendship of people like this, which is the foundation of everything good in human society.

The Gospel
According to John

Introduction

As we have looked at the first three Gospels I have been all too
aware that sometimes I have repeated myself – given the fact that
I'm an old man now, that isn't surprising. I have tried to remove
some of these repetitions but in part they are inescapable.
Matthew, Mark and Luke use so much of the same material.

John's Gospel is quite different from all of the rest. It may or
may not have some connection with the apostle John, often
thought of as the disciple Jesus loved best – a concept which
raises problems of its own. How could a perfect man, such as
Jesus is supposed to be, have preferences or favourites?

John's Gospel omits all birth *stories*; the baptism and
temptation of Jesus; the Last Supper, Gethsemane and the
Ascension. There are no parables. No one with devils or evil
spirits is healed. Does John have no memory of these things or
does he leave them out because they have been dealt with by
others? How significant are these things? Or is John just less
concerned to tell the story of Jesus and more concerned with
theology, philosophy and meditation?

I shall make no attempt to discuss these questions or to study
questions of date and authorship, I am solely concerned with
considering the text as it is. What does this Gospel actually say
and what does it say to me now?

Chapter One

1–18: From the very first words of this Gospel we are taken from the world of the Bible into the world of Greek philosophy and into 'one of the greatest adventures of religious thought ever achieved by the mind of man.' (William Barclay)

The claim that Jesus is more than just another human being reaches its fullest exposition in the Gospels right here. John's Gospel is sometimes called 'the spiritual Gospel'. Certainly there is nothing crude about the theology we find here. It is not too much to say that our whole attitude to Jesus hangs finally on our acceptance or rejection of the teachings of this chapter.

When John speaks of Jesus as 'the Word' he is linking the Genesis account of creation with the Old Testament idea of 'wisdom' and with the Greek concept of the logos. There are similarities between ancient Greek thought and Hinduism.

The ancient Greeks had many gods. So does Hinduism. A Brahmin I knew once told me, 'we have many gods for uneducated people but in reality we focus on very few like you Christians'! Thoughtful Greeks had no real religious belief in most of their gods. They either disposed of them more or less completely, or they spiritualised the idea of God, turning divinity into a kind of philosophical idea – as both Hindus and Buddhists have done. But this kind of deity becomes so remote that there is virtually no possible connection between it and ourselves. And so an intermediary is needed, still divine but within reach.

Hindus have several intermediaries, notably Krishna. For the Jews this was the divine wisdom. For the Greeks it was the logos, the Word. The logos was 'the creating and the guiding and the directing power of God which made the universe and which keeps the universe going.' (Barclay) As I put it in my own *An Unbeliever's Guide to the Bible*:

> These Greeks saw the Word as the unifying principle behind the universe, that which sustains and holds the universe together. Having linked these two concepts, John goes on to join the two with the incarnation of Jesus.
>
> The Gospel claims that Jesus is the Word and that the Word is God. It claims that as God, Jesus was responsible for the creation

of the world ('without him was not anything made that was made').

'. . .and the Word became flesh and dwelt among us.' The divine Jesus became a man. As man, Jesus has made God known to us.

It is a breathtaking proposition and has always been an inspiration to Christian philosophers and theologians but is it true? The Genesis account of creation on which part of it is based, is certainly not true. Nevertheless, the idea of some sort of creator is a hypothesis that is not necessarily destroyed by evolutionary theory.

It must also be said that the idea of a unifying principle behind the universe (some great ultimate Mind) is another hypothesis that has always commended itself to many people.

The idea that this Ultimate Mind, this Creative Principle, could become a man really is intellectually exciting in the same way as a great symphony heard for the first time is overwhelming in its power. It led Christians to develop their idea of Jesus as both Perfect God and Perfect Man. But see what follows from this:

If he is God he is beyond criticism. If he is PERFECT man he is also beyond criticism, but is he really a man? Are humans not, by their very nature, imperfect? Doesn't the idea of perfection actually take away something of the humanity of Jesus?

It certainly undermines the critical faculties of Christians. They find it extraordinarily difficult to say or to listen to anything that is in any way critical of Jesus. For many years after I left Christianity I shared that difficulty. If you believe in Jesus as God, there is no escaping that problem. But if, in spite of the overwhelming force of the intellectual and philosophical ideas of incarnation theology, you finally reject both the idea of Jesus as God, and the idea of his perfection, then you can finally examine him simply as another human being.

That will transform your approach to him.

And yet, if you are an ex-Christian, as I am, you will still have lurking hesitations and it will still bring you pain whenever you criticise the man you have worshipped. There is no easy way past this problem. My own way past may be of help to others:

We do not actually know Jesus! All we have are pictures painted by his disciples. We have no means of knowing how far those pictures are accurate. We have no means of knowing how

131

true the Gospels are. When we left my school a little record of our schooldays appeared in the school magazine. I read my paragraph eagerly, only to be disappointed at inaccuracies and things that were left out which seemed important to me. If Jesus could read the Gospels how appalled would he be at the image of him found there?

When I criticise 'Jesus' in the pages ahead, as I shall do, it is important to recognise that I am not actually criticising Jesus himself. I've no idea how far he deserves my criticisms. What I am criticising is the portrait or image of Jesus handed down by his followers. As we shall see, that is an image that is thoroughly flawed. Whether as a man or as a teacher and healer, the 'Jesus' shown to us, for all his qualities, which are many, leaves a great deal to be desired. I have found it difficult to write these things but I feel that they NEED to be written.

For me Jesus was just another human being, as fallible as the rest of us. It looks as though he was a man of some grace or charm and he clearly had qualities which made people want to follow him, but he is far from being the only person to have had those kind of qualities.

It is time to turn to the text of John itself.

1–5 and 9–15: These verses spell out everything I have been trying to say. For those of us who are familiar with them, they are some of the finest and most exciting words we have ever read. Their power is immense and their message utterly thrilling:

'The light shines in the darkness, and the darkness has not overcome it.' (v. 5)

For John, through the darkness of the crucifixion: For me and for many of you, through the darkness of the Second World War; through the darkness of all the massacres, ethnic cleansings, revolutions, wars, oppressions; and through all of our personal human tragedies; the light of Jesus and his Gospel continues to shine. What a triumphant, exhilarating, inspiring, liberating message.

Is it any wonder that I found it so hard to move on from Christianity? Perhaps it only became possible because I firmly believe that Jesus or no Jesus, Gospel or no Gospel, there is always light to be found. In the very darkest moments of life and in the very darkest human experiences, light shines. In my own darkest hours that light came from Christians and non-Christians alike – but mostly from non-Christians. The light of human nature at its best confronts human nature at its worst, and calamity and tragedy at their worst, and goes on shining.

14–18: John pinpoints two characteristics of Jesus the 'Word made flesh': 'grace and truth'. These are also to be two supreme characteristics of the Gospel, the message of Jesus: 'grace and truth'.

You couldn't have anything much more attractive. John claims, as many of his fellow Christians would claim, 'from his fullness we have all received, grace upon grace.' (v. 16)

I would have made the same claim. In fact, I would still make that claim because I am well aware that I owe an immense debt to my Christian upbringing and background. I suspect that if my fellow non-Christians could distinguish between the Christian Church as an institution and Jesus and his message, they might share my respect for the latter. But I want to go further than respect and gratitude – further than the Christian Gospel.

'Grace and truth' are not the exclusive property of Christians, nor are they only given through the Christian Gospel. They are not in the exclusive gift of the Church. Wherever human beings are to be found, 'grace and truth' may be found as well.

6–8 and 15: Interwoven with all this there are references to John the Baptist as the prophet who points people in the direction of Jesus. John was older than Jesus so his claim that Jesus 'ranks before me, for he was before me', only makes sense if Jesus is seen as 'the Word. . . in the beginning with God.' John follows these references with a fuller account of John's ministry than any of the other Gospels.

19–28: John explains that his prophetic ministry is all about preparing people for Jesus.

29–34: Although, according to the other Gospels, John and Jesus were cousins, John claims that he didn't know that Jesus was the man he was looking for until he saw the Holy Spirit descend on him.

I have already commented on the descent elsewhere but there is a new element here. John calls Jesus, 'the Lamb of God, who takes away the sin of the world'. (v. 29)

There is surprisingly little in the other Gospels about sin and sacrifice which is why, when you read them, it is so difficult to see why Jesus thought that his death on the cross was necessary. Here, right at the outset, John sets out his stall. These words define the ministry of Jesus. He is not just a teacher or a healer. He came to offer himself as a sacrifice, as a saviour to free us all from our sin.

When verse 29 speaks of 'the sin of the world', it means the sin of all of us.

I no longer acknowledge that there is such a thing as sin. By definition, sin is something wrong which we have done to God. If there is no such thing as a god, then there is no such thing as sin. There is wrong-doing – oh yes, plenty of that, but not sin.

But I wouldn't want that paragraph to deflect us from a proper study of this important verse in John. In the Jewish temple and in many other religions, 'sin' was dealt with by offering sacrifices of farm produce, birds or animals. That practice is now to be rendered obsolete. One perfect sacrifice is to be made which will be sufficient to bring salvation for all the world – universally and for all time. And Jesus is that sacrifice.

For many centuries that was one of the central doctrines of the Christian church and especially of the Protestant Evangelical wing of the church. But it is a doctrine which has always given trouble to Christian theologians. And for many years a very dear friend of mine ensured that it gave trouble to me. She forced me to study the best theologians of my day to try to find a way past the repulsion she felt. In particular she hated the old evangelical glorying in 'the blood of the Lamb'. The very mention of it would send congregations into cries and sighs: 'A...men Lord. Jee...sus.'

My friend Betty hated all that glorying in the 'blood' and so did I. Did that mean that the sacrifice of Jesus had to go out of the window too? I tried so hard to show her that it didn't. The fact that I never succeeded probably means that I didn't fully manage to convince myself!

After all, how could any decent father require such a sacrifice from his son? And how could such a sacrifice have any meaning for anyone other than the person who died? I know that many Christians believe that the sacrifice of Jesus has saved them from sin. And I know all the ways in which Christians claim that it can and does.

I wrestled with all those claims and studied the traditional

134

answers to my questions. But ultimately none of the answers satisfied me. When a man gives his life saving another man from drowning, that is a sacrifice which saves. But it doesn't seem to me that there is any remote likeness between that and the sacrifice on the cross.

The fact that Jesus thought of it as a sacrifice may inspire a man to gratitude and may inspire him to change his way of life. So Jesus may 'save' a man in that way. But there is no way in which his sacrifice can cancel 'the sin of the world'.

It is also right at the beginning of John's Gospel that we are told that Jesus 'is the Son of God'. (v. 34) So, right at the outset, all the supreme claims are made and in the process we are confronted with all the intricacies of the Christian conception of God as a Trinity: three persons, one God. It all makes me wonder whether the Christian Gospel is as universal as it cracks up to be.

Is it possible that the philosophical idea of the Word is beyond most of us? Is it possible that the intricacies of the Christian doctrine of salvation are beyond most of us? Is it possible that the unfathomable mystery of the doctrine of the Trinity is beyond most of us? Is this, in fact, just a Gospel for intellectuals and academics rather than something for ordinary people like me? For a Gospel really to be 'good news', which is what the word Gospel means, it must be accessible for everyone. We must all be able to understand it to fathom it, to grasp it and to rejoice in it. It must never be beyond us – even if it is always enticing us to reach beyond the place we have reached already.

I mustn't allow myself to be diverted too far or for too long, but at the time when some Greeks were coming up with their philosophy of the Word there were others whose thinking led them into much simpler paths. People like Epicurus focussed on the simple pleasures of life and on the power of ordinary human friendship to break down all the barriers between people. Centuries before Jesus he was showing to us that every human being had the same value as every other human being. Young, old, rich, poor, slave, free, native or foreigner, male or female, everybody was welcome without distinction.

But we must return to John's Gospel:

35–42: The story of the first followers of Jesus is different from the story told in the other Gospels and seems more authentic. They were men who began by following John the

Baptist and, with his encouragement, switched their allegiance. And it is here that we learn that it was self-effacing Andrew who brought his brother Simon Peter to Jesus. Having done so, he more or less disappears from sight. I have always liked this story and always liked Andrew too!

43–51: Two more followers who probably knew Andrew and Peter and who came from their town, come to Jesus. Jesus' comment to Nathaniel is baffling to us as we hurry indoors out of the cold. But the climate is different in Palestine. Jesus had obviously seen Nathaniel either in prayer or in quiet thought or meditation, sitting in the shade of his fig tree. So yet another fig tree features in the Gospel story!

But what are we to make of verse 51? Does it have any concrete meaning? Does it point forward to the vision of the Transfiguration and was Nathaniel one of the few who were there? John certainly was, but was that John also the author of the Gospel?

Chapter Two

1–11: **The marriage at Cana in Galilee.**

There are very few miracles in John's Gospel and each of them is regarded as a 'sign' to teach us something.

The dialogue is obviously not authentic (how would it be?). Mary, the mother of Jesus, is not at all put out by his apparently curt response to her request.

Whether we believe the story of this miracle or not, what is the sign within the story? Is it hidden in verse 10 and does it suggest that everything on offer from the predecessors of Jesus was like poor wine compared with what he has to offer?

Verse 12 shows that his relationship with his own family was still a good one – but it is typical of the time and typical of the Gospels that there is no mention of his sisters.

13–25: John moves the story of the cleansing of the temple forward to the beginning of his story. This is in line with all the other things he has spelt out at the beginning, things the other Gospels suggest were only revealed over time. Their gradual revelation would seem to be the more likely.

With the cleansing of the temple comes confrontation and words taken to be about his resurrection – once more something that is not mentioned until fairly late on in the other Gospels.

Chapter Three

1–15: Right through to verse 21, this is a crucially important chapter for Christians. Reading it again, I'm not sure whether most of them are aware of how crucial it is or of what it actually says. Does familiarity blunt our understanding and our sensitivities?

Verses 1–15 focus on the words 'you must be born anew.' There are no half measures. Either people are born anew and enter into the family of God – the chosen people of God – or they remain outside. They 'cannot enter the kingdom of God.' (v. 5)

The message is as clear as can be even though Nicodemus is unable to take it on board. I don't imagine that he failed to understand. I suspect that he understood very clearly but he couldn't accept such teaching. In or out; black or white; accepted or condemned – is that really how we are to see life and human society?

Jesus claimed that, if we are to enter into the kingdom of God we all need a new, spiritual birth akin to our human birth. We need to be born of 'water and the Spirit.'

I wonder if this is Jesus speaking or the early church? People have always entered the church by baptism with water. Was the church already beginning to claim that you couldn't enter the kingdom of God without being baptised? It is a claim that has led to considerable difficulties. Roman Catholics used to exclude all babies who were not baptised and place them in 'limbo'. Although they have changed their teaching there are still a few who rush to baptise sickly babies just to be on the safe side. What a dreadful idea this is: that God could not accept and welcome children without a drop of water and a few magic words.

Christians themselves are deeply divided over baptism. Should children be baptised or should baptism be reserved for those who know what they are doing and who know the meaning of baptism by the Spirit? Should it, in fact, be reserved for those who have already been baptised by the Spirit? Or does believers' baptism bring baptism with the Spirit with it?

And what of those who somehow slip through the net? My father was a devoted and faithful Christian but was never baptised with water. Was he excluded when his time came?

All these things are problems for Christians but not for the rest of us.

16–24: Verse sixteen and the following verses mean more to many Christians than perhaps any verses in the whole of the New Testament. But I wonder whether they realise just how much these verses imply or just how deeply they divide society into two.

For verse 16 to become meaningful it is first of all necessary to believe in God. More than that, it is necessary to believe in God as Christians see him. It is also necessary to believe that the human Jesus is in some unique sense the Son of God. Other people may become the children of God but not in the same way that Jesus is the Son of God 'who descended from heaven'. (v. 13)

Given those two beliefs it becomes possible to believe that those who put their faith in him are saved from sin for all eternity. But that involves people in rather a lot of additional beliefs:

belief in ourselves as evil sinners needing salvation;
belief in everlasting judgement – a judgement which
     divides believers from the rest of us completely;
belief in Jesus as a Saviour from sin;
belief in life after death for the chosen in an eternity of bliss;
and finally, belief in the condemnation of all the rest of us!

I wonder how many Christians who love that passage are aware of all those things or of the gulf that is supposed to exist between them and the rest of us because they have seen the light and we haven't. Such condemnation simply for failing to believe seems pretty vicious to me.

We are certainly all fallible – some more than others. But in my experience, most people go through life doing their best and living their lives as well as they can. I know that a few of us are pretty nasty characters and rather more are weak and easily led astray, but it is only a few of us.

If members of either of these latter two groups can be changed for the better, whether by Jesus or by anyone else – and it does sometimes happen – then that is wonderful. But it is wonderful *now*. I have no belief at all in everlasting judgement or life after death come to that. For good or ill, we do our living now.

22–30: This is the only Gospel which speaks of Jesus baptising people. Did he, or is this another example of the early church trying to underline the importance of baptism? According to this story, people compared the baptisms of John and Jesus and wondered whether John felt that Jesus had the authority to baptise.

John's reply is highly significant. 'What matters in baptism is not who performs the rite but what is given from heaven.' (v. 27)

John goes on to play down his own importance and to stress the importance of Jesus. 'He must increase, but I must decrease,' (v. 30) In spite of that, there were still communities of followers of John the Baptist quite a number of centuries into the Christian era.

31–36: Are these still the words of John the Baptist or are they the words of the Gospel writer? They build on the claims already made for Jesus, laying claim upon claim rather like rungs in a ladder. And they end once more by dividing humanity into two:

'He who believes in the Son has eternal life;'

'the wrath of God rests upon' everyone else.

Even when I was a Christian I couldn't accept that God could be wrathful like that. Now, of course, I don't believe in God at all or in these claims made for Jesus.

Chapter Four

1–3: The first two verses are very curious. 'The Lord' and 'Jesus' seem to be two distinct people. The Lord causes Jesus to move from Judaea to Galilee so that his ministry is not viewed as being in competition with John's.

And then there is a strange correction in verse two. In verse 22 of the previous chapter we were told that Jesus remained in Judaea with his disciples 'and baptised'. Now we are told that 'Jesus himself did not baptise'.

It looks as though some of the followers of John the Baptist had taken up his ministry and were themselves preaching and baptising when Jesus came along. They continued for a while before becoming full time followers of Jesus. We can't really know and none of this is particularly significant. But, as I have already mentioned, there were followers of John the Baptist who continued his ministry for centuries.

3–15: 'Give me a drink.' Am I doing Jesus an injustice if I say that that sounds pretty discourteous? The fact that there is no 'please' may just be a linguistic thing. My Aramaic is not up to telling us but I once had to learn a language that had no real word for please or thank you.

But the significance of this is that Jesus spoke to a Samaritan at a time when the Jews had 'no dealings with Samaritans.' How horrible such attitudes are. How is it that humans can be so unkind and divisive? Racial and religious discrimination and division are still prevalent and still deep rooted. They are vile, obnoxious and just plain wrong.

But Jesus does not simply speak to a Samaritan, he speaks to a Samaritan WOMAN! How extraordinary is that? It was pretty extraordinary and way ahead of its time in that part of the world. Yet, several hundred years earlier in Greece, as I have mentioned, Epicurus had been welcoming people into his garden regardless of who they were, what their sex, status or age, and all on equal terms of simple human friendship.

The conversation between Jesus and the woman followed a series of misunderstandings through which the author shows Jesus as the one who offers a teaching like 'a spring of water welling up to eternal life.'

16–26: Although the woman assumed that Jesus had special powers and insight to know so much about her, it wasn't necessarily so. The facts of her marital life are stated but not commented on. Apart from convincing her that Jesus is a prophet they are quite irrelevant to all that follows.

The conversation about worship in Jerusalem and 'on this mountain' refers back to old history and to the causes of the enmity between Jews and Samaritans – a rather nasty history told in the Old Testament where the Jews rejected Samaritan help on narrow, rigid, racial grounds. After centuries those divisive positions had only hardened and grown deeper – and the attitudes continue to this day. Nor was Jesus free from prejudice:

'We' (Jews) 'worship what we know.' The clear implication is that ALL other worship is based on ignorance and error. Although Jesus was talking about the Samaritans, his exclusiveness would have applied to such sophisticated religions and philosophies as Hinduism, Buddhism, Confucianism and Taoism, let alone the thinking of the ancient Greeks.

This is breathtaking in its arrogance and intolerance. As if only the Jews, who at this time were still sacrificing birds and animals in their Temple worship, could know the truth and the right way to worship!

When Christians focus on the following verses they conveniently overlook the fact that that is where Jesus begins. The move forward from all of that IS both new and special in Palestine, but the teaching of Jesus had already been matched in other religious philosophies, perhaps most notably in Buddhism and Taoism. This is not to deny that in these verses Jesus reaches a pinnacle of religious teaching:

> '. . .true worshippers will worship the Father in spirit and truth, for such the Father seeks to worship him. God is spirit, and those who worship him must worship in spirit and truth.' (vvs 23–24)

A pinnacle of RELIGIOUS teaching, yes, but for those of us who have no gods or religion, a teaching which has no meaning at all.

This passage ends with Jesus' claim that he is the Messiah. Perhaps the loveliest thing about this whole story is the fact that some of the most sublime teaching Jesus ever gave was given in a one to one conversation with a despised foreigner and a woman – and what a woman!

27–30: No wonder the disciples marvelled.

31–38: There are simple facts in this passage about the way the adrenalin rush of certain kinds of work or activity can make food and drink seem quite irrelevant and unnecessary for a time.

But Jesus also sees the work of the prophets of old as preparing a harvest for him and for his disciples. Different periods of history and changing social conditions do always seem to be in part, preparing the way for something else. We speak of ideas 'whose time has come' or 'not yet come' and of people who are 'before their time'. No age is static. Things are always moving on and every age both builds on and destroys the past while itself preparing for the future.

39–45: Jesus stayed for two highly successful days with the Samaritans and then moved into Galilee where his success continued.

46–54: Cana had been the scene of the first 'sign'. Now Capernaum became the scene of the second, a healing at distance through faith.

Random thoughts written sometime after this commentary:

Somewhere I have mentioned the girl who said to me, 'Why are they always trying to make us feel bad about ourselves?'

A great deal of religion is about power. If the church can convince us that we are sinners and that salvation can only be found through the church, then the church has power over us. I don't think many in the church consciously think like that, but that is how it works out.

Alongside that I found myself thinking about something I had written (relating to John chapter 16?) about the fact that we are always turning to the teachers of ancient times as if they alone can show us how to live.

Why do we imagine that because someone has studied Greek and perhaps Hebrew, and some ancient books including the teaching of the prophets and of Jesus, he is somehow equipped to teach us about LIFE.

And then, suddenly, I found myself asking, why do we imagine that a thirty year old bachelor, a self-appointed teacher, can tell us more about life than a woman who has had five husbands and who is living out of wedlock with number six?

Do we know why she has had five husbands or is living with number six? Has the bachelor really any right to tell her to 'go and sin no more'? (In part I am doing him an injustice. After all, she took no offence at what he said and was so impressed by him that she told others about him, but that doesn't alter my general drift.)

Recently a barmaid was talking to me about an alcoholic. Even though I know full well that alcoholism is an illness; and that many people with addictions are people of great sensitivity and quality; I viewed this particular man with distaste. But she knew him. She told me what a lovely man he was. It was a real eye-opener and I came away thoroughly chastened.

None of us has the right or is in a position to look down our moral noses at anyone else or to judge anyone else.

Chapter Five

1–18: In the other Gospels Jesus only went to Jerusalem at the end of his ministry. This Gospel moves him around a good deal more. This visit to Jerusalem led to the claim that God was his father and gave the authorities two grounds for hostility to him:

    i: He broke the sabbath law;

    ii He claimed a special and unique relationship with God, a relationship which made him 'equal with God'.

19–29: These verses confirm the claim that Jesus is equal with God.

25–29: The final verses of this section contain the basis for the Christian teaching that after his death Jesus went and preached to the dead. This was a primitive attempt to show that God is scrupulously fair and to answer the question, if the Christian Gospel is universal, what happens to all those who came before Jesus and what happens to all those who go through life without ever hearing the Gospel?

It IS a primitive attempt at an answer and thoroughly inadequate and unsatisfactory. But even within its own limits it is unsatisfactory. It claims that when Jesus preached to the dead, 'some who have done good' found 'the resurrection of life' whilst others who 'have done evil' found 'judgement'.

But you can't divide people so simply into two camps. None of us is completely good and none of us is completely evil. We are all a mixture of both and any simplistic judgement would be thoroughly unjust in spite of Jesus' claim to the contrary (v. 30).

30–47: Jesus sets out his claims here, claims that would not make him very popular with the Jewish authorities:

'Moses wrote of me.' (v. 46)

'The scriptures bear witness to me.' (v. 39)

John the Baptist 'was a burning and shining lamp. . . but the testimony which I have is greater than John.' (vvs. 35–36)

My works 'bear me witness that the Father has sent me.' (v. 36)

'The Father who sent me has himself borne witness to me.' (v. 37)

To his hearers these were immense claims to make but whether we think they have any real meaning is another thing altogether.

Chapter Six

1–15: The feeding of the five thousand.

This is the only 'miracle' recorded in all four Gospels. It clearly made a huge impression.

16–21: Jesus walking on the sea.

Recorded as fact, for me this passage marked the significant moment in my own life when I woke up to another fact: the fact that I neither believed in this miracle nor in any other.

22–40: This 'remembers' in a fairly artificially constructed message the teaching Jesus drew from his feeding of the 5,000.

Verse 27 is of importance for those who believe in 'eternal life' but it has a wider relevance, calling us all to try to distinguish between the things that matter in life and the things that have no lasting significance.

The central claim of the whole passage is in verse 35. It is the first of a series of claims in this Gospel, the famous 'I am' claims. They lead Jesus to call on people to believe in him. In verse 27 he has said that people should believe in him. Now he underlines it:

'I am the bread of life; he who comes to me shall not hunger, and he who believes in me shall never thirst.' (v. 35)

These words have nothing to do with ordinary food and drink. They are all about nourishing the soul or our spiritual life. So for Christians verses 35 to 40 are crucially important and wonderfully inspiring. That makes it all the harder for those of us who consider that the words 'soul' and 'spiritual' are meaningless to comment.

41–51: To those who criticised his teaching at the time, Jesus could do no other than repeat and underline it: 'he who believes has eternal life. I am the bread of life. . . and the bread which I shall give for the life of the world is my flesh.' (verses 47, 48 & 51)

If Jesus really said these things, he was already aware of the end which awaited him but he had supreme confidence in himself and in his Father – God. There is no hint of uncertainty or doubt.

'I am the bread of life.' 'The work of God' for all of *us* is simply to 'believe'.

But it is clear that some of those who heard him did not believe.

52–59: These verses are not just a further exposition of all that he has been saying. They are an exposition of the meaning of the central Christian rite known as the Mass, the Eucharist or Holy Communion, a rite derived from the Last Supper which has not yet taken place.

This makes it clear that we should not regard John's Gospel as a sequential, historical account of the ministry of Jesus. It is more of a meditation on the meaning of that ministry.

As we have seen in the other Gospels, many Christians take verses 53–56 absolutely literally. They claim that every time they share in their central Christian rite, the bread and the wine are miraculously changed into the body and blood of Jesus so that when they eat the bread and drink the wine they really are eating his flesh and drinking his blood.

I find that concept utterly appalling. So do many Christians. These claim that the bread and wine REPRESENT the body and blood of Jesus. Their central rite is a remembering of the sacrifice of Jesus on the cross, an act of faith and communion with the risen Jesus, and an expression of their fellowship with one another.

This is an approach which any unbeliever can appreciate. It takes the ordinary human qualities of hospitality, social interaction, friendship and fellowship and turns them into a memorable religious rite. Those of us who do not believe in Jesus or share in this sacrament do well to remember the human qualities on which it is based and to express them in our own lives.

60–71: Even some of his close disciples felt that Jesus was going over the top in the claims he made for himself and 'many of his disciples drew back and no longer went about with him.' This led Jesus to ask the twelve if they were also going to leave him. After Peter's declaration of faith, Jesus said:

'Did I not choose you, the twelve, and one of you is a devil.' (v. 70)

That little statement undermines all of Jesus' claims in this chapter. Either his choice of Judas reveals a serious failure in his assessment of Judas in the first place. Or, and this is far worse, he chose Judas deliberately, knowing that Judas would end up betraying him and quite prepared to put Judas through all that that would mean for him.

Either way, this man who makes such immense claims for himself, is found seriously wanting.

Chapter Seven

There is an unaccountable dithering and uncertainty about Jesus in the early stages of this chapter. The whole chapter is at pains to show how he divided and polarised people's opinions. 'Even his brothers did not believe in him.' (v. 5)

145

g

His brothers urged him to go to Jerusalem for the Jewish feast of Tabernacles so that he could make himself better known. He told them that he wasn't going.

But then he went privately. Did he deliberately deceive them or did he just change his mind? And then did he change it again when he turned a private visit into a public one?

Verses 23–24 refer back to the healing in chapter 5. The main teaching of the chapter is in verses 37–39.

Chapter Eight
(to be precise: chapter 7:53 to 8:11)

It is fairly well known now that the four Gospels were not the only Gospels to be written. In the early centuries after the life of Jesus there were all sorts of stories told about him and many of them were written down.

In some modern translations of the Gospels you will find John 7, 53–8, 11 missing and then included as a postscript after the rest of the Gospel; or you will find it in small print included almost as a footnote. This is because it was no part of the original Gospel. It was one of those floating stories.

As the early church began to sift through all the material it had on Jesus, it slowly settled on the four Gospels we have been studying as the ones that could be given a seal of approval and included in the New Testament. But someone, or several someones, felt that this little story was too good to lose. So, when he was copying out his own copy of John's Gospel – copied by hand, of course, since there was no printing, he slipped this story in. Other people copied his copy including the insert, and so the story became part of the Gospel as we know it. The chapter and verse numbers came much later.

In modern times scholars have done a great deal of detective work on ancient manuscripts and they discovered that this story was no part of the original manuscript.

That bothered them so much that they decided to relegate it either to a footnote or to a postscript. It is sad that they have felt it necessary to do so for it is one of the most attractive and one of the loveliest stories of Jesus in the whole of the New Testament. Whoever inserted it knew what he was doing. It is a story which needs no exposition. It just cries out to be read.

I understand that modern Sharia (Moslem) law is the same as the old Mosaic Law. No one asks why anyone commits adultery, or whether it really is so serious after all. There is just a blanket condemnation but notice that it is only the women who are stoned.

But who would ever be stoned if it was only 'that one who is faultless' who threw the stones? Notice also part of Jesus' final comment: 'Has no one condemned you? No more do I.'

In Gospels that are full of judgement, division between good and bad, rewards and punishments, that is wonderfully refreshing. No wonder that anonymous old Christian kept this story. (In fact, more than one kept it, for it turns up in other places in other old manuscripts.) There is a lot of the New Testament I can happily discard but this story is one that I shall always treasure.

12–20: Here is the second of the famous 'I am' claims:

'I am the light of the world; he who follows me will not walk in darkness, but will have the light of life.' (v. 12)

To the Christian that sounds absolutely wonderful and when the Pharisees challenge Jesus, Christians go along with all that Jesus says. But what is it that he does say?

He says that his claims are authenticated by God and that his opponents do not know God so they can't authenticate his claim. Many religious arguments depend on the same kind of logic.

But just suppose for one moment that there is no God. The whole argument falls to the ground and we are left with the Pharisees' criticism, 'You are bearing witness to yourself.' If there is no God, that is precisely what Jesus is doing.

I'm quite sure that Jesus believed what he said and his words certainly thrill and inspire disciples who also believe them. But just suppose that the Pharisees were right. What follows?

There is no doubt that some of the actions of Jesus, as in the story we have just read, bring light into all sorts of dark corners. And there is no doubt that a great deal of his teaching does the same. But that is as far as it goes.

Jesus may well be a light in the world but he is only one of many. And if he thinks that he is more than that; if he thinks that he is the only light; then he is not only misguided but he is perhaps also beginning to lose his grip on reality. We should

147

perhaps pay rather more attention than we usually do, to the Pharisees.

21–30: To an unbeliever these verses only underline the questions or suspicions of my last paragraph above. And they call in question Christian teaching about the real humanity of this man.

If he is really so different from all the rest of us, then he is not a genuine man. And what does it mean, to die in our sins? We all die in our sins and in our virtues too. When we die, it is the person who has lived who dies – neither saint nor sinner but a bit of both.

Jesus and many of his followers believe in life after death. Many of us don't – certainly not on these terms. As creatures of the animal kingdom, we live and we die and that is all that there is to it. There is no need for a great song and dance about it all. It is all very simple. So while we live let us make the most of our lives, living them out in warmth of friendship and in depth of love. And when our time comes let us hope that we leave a few happy memories behind.

31–38: Jesus claims that we are all slaves to sin and that it is only if we follow his teaching that we shall know the truth and find freedom.

But we are not all slaves to sin. Some of us – comparatively few – are slaves to some kind of addiction. And all of us think things and do things that are wrong sometimes. But the religious focus on sin is both wrong and unhealthy. In fact, it is often positively harmful, leaving perfectly decent people riddled with feelings of guilt and unworthiness and filling them with unspeakable fears.

THAT is the truth and it is THAT truth which really can set people free – free to be themselves, fallible and imperfect but also wonderful and quite unique.

39–47: These verses only underline all that I have been saying. Jesus condemns people wholesale, claiming 'you are of your father the devil'. (v. 44) How can anyone say such a thing?

There is no denying that, at our worst, we can be pretty awful, and this is particularly true of mobs. But break a mob down. Separate it into individuals. Examine each individual. There are a few, a tiny few, who perhaps deserve Jesus' strictures. But most people have been swept away by a host of different thoughts, motives, emotions. Some of them will remember with boastfulness but many more will remember with shame.

There is nothing in John's Gospel up to this point which justifies Jesus' blanket condemnation. He almost sounds as though he despises them all. If he did, then he has fallen pretty low himself.

48–59: The provocation of the words of Jesus led finally to the kind of mob violence of which I have spoken, but it almost seems as though Jesus has invited that. He calls them all liars and makes, what must have seemed to all of them, outrageous claims for himself. Even if those claims were true, there is no justification for the way in which Jesus has spoken.

The claims themselves are all a part of the foundations on which Christians build their theology of Jesus as God, one of the three persons of the Trinity. In this chapter, again and again Jesus claims that his own relationship with the Father is unique and his deeds are those of God; and that he shared in the life of God throughout eternity – 'before Abraham was, I am'.

Even Christian believers will surely recognise that this is pretty incendiary stuff. The claims Jesus made in this chapter drove a wedge between himself and the whole of the rest of humanity.

Chapter Nine

1–12: **Some strange and primitive ideas.**
A man was born blind. It was assumed that the blindness was the result of sin, either that of his parents or, incredibly, his own!

What is it that leads people to have such extraordinary ideas or to make such extraordinary assumptions? Jesus puts them right but then makes a claim that is absolutely dreadful: the man was born blind SO THAT 'the works of God might be made manifest in him.'

It would be a pretty awful god who imposed such a thing as blindness on a newborn baby simply so that, at a later stage, he could heal the blindness.

This particular blindness seemed to respond to remarkably basic treatment. But it is perhaps a useful reminder that a great deal of the blindness in the world DOES respond to very simple and comparatively cheap treatment. By supporting medical charities we can all share in giving people their sight back.

13–34: Because the healing was done on a sabbath there were serious repercussions. The account is worth reading for some of the marvellous moments it has in the confrontation between the man who had been healed and the Pharisees:

'This man [Jesus] is a sinner.'

'Whether he is a sinner, I do not know; one thing I know, that though I was blind, now I see.'

'We know that God has spoken to Moses, but as for this man, we do not know where he comes from.'

'Why this is a marvel! You do not know where he comes from, and yet he opened my eyes. . . Never since the world began has it been heard that anyone opened the eyes of a man born blind.'

(vvs. 24, 25, 29, 30)

35–41: When Jesus heard that the man had been cast out of the synagogue (the equivalent of excommunication) he sought him out. Clearly Jesus felt that faith in him was more important than membership of the synagogue. The chapter ends with significant words about seeing and not seeing; the blindness of intransigence.

Chapter Ten

1–48: Almost every verse of this passage is memorable and valuable for the Christian. It contains two more of the famous 'I am' claims; 'I am the door of the sheep'(fold) and 'I am the good shepherd'.

For the Christian this is a marvellous passage. It gives a wonderful sense of belonging; of the loving care of the Good Shepherd; of his willingness to give himself completely for his sheep and for those 'other sheep' who are still to be gathered in. It also expresses his relationship with his Father.

At first sight it is such a lovely and valued passage that it seems shameful to criticise it and yet it does actually lay itself open to a good deal of criticism.

4: Jesus is the shepherd whose sheep follow him. Whereas English shepherds drive their sheep, in many countries shepherds lead theirs.

But the image paints us as sheep with no mind or will of our own. We are just people who follow our leader as part of a flock with no independent identity worthy of the name. There is nothing more dangerous in human society than this thoughtless tendency to follow a leader, as history has shown us again and again.

8: 'All who came before me are thieves and robbers.'

This is a pretty damning criticism of the Old Testament prophets and teachers, and in Christian hands it has often become a damning criticism of all religious and ethical teachers other than their own. There is one way and only one; one religion and only one. At best all the rest are inadequate and at worst they are false and only able to lead people astray.

We have only to take time to discover the riches contained in the teaching of other religions and philosophies to learn that Christians have no exclusive hold on things of value or on truth.

12–13: Jesus doesn't think very highly of 'the hirelings'. Only the owner will take proper care of his sheep to the point of laying down his life for his sheep.

I know that we shouldn't make too much of one passage and that there are others where he speaks of good and faithful servants. But I can't help thinking of all those poor shepherds down through the ages, out on the hills caring for the sheep while their owner is safely tucked up in bed with his wife at home. I've been an employer and know how important it is to have proper respect for those who work for you.

16: 'There shall be one flock' or if you like 'one holy, catholic and apostolic church'.

The flock is not one flock and the church has never been one or holy or catholic or apostolic. We walk the hills near home and there are sheep scattered all over the hillside bleating like hell, all with different voices. That is my image of the Christian Church. The only thing the sheep have in common is their owner.

17–18: 'I lay down my life, that I may take it again. . . I have power to lay it down, and I have power to take it again.'

How much meaning does his sacrifice have if, having laid down his life he has 'power to take it again'? Doesn't the resurrection actually undermine the meaning and the reality of the crucifixion?

19–21: It seems that no one has heard a word he has been saying. They all hark back to the healing of the blind man.

22–42: Jesus is still thinking about the image of sheep and shepherd but his claims are pretty clear.

He believed himself to be the Christ, the Messiah, the Saviour, although not the political Christ they were looking for.

151

And he believed that he had a unique relationship with God:

'I and the Father are one.'

To the Jews that second claim was blasphemy and deserving of death. Faced with their charge Jesus pointed to the good things he was doing which they could surely see were 'the works of my Father.' (v. 37)

However much I may criticise him, I have no wish to deny the quality of much of his teaching or the value to the recipients of many of the things he did. But that is a long way short of acknowledging that his claims for himself are true.

Chapter Eleven

1–44: The raising of Lazarus.

This is quite a story – as a story. But why is it that stories like this so often leave uncomfortable questions, even for those who believe them?

'Lord, he whom you love is ill.'
'This illness is not unto death; it is for the glory of God.' (vvs. 3–4)

Was Jesus right? If so, then Lazarus was not really raised from death. Or was he wrong, in which case he was fallible and therefore not divine.

5–6: 'Jesus loved Martha and her sister and Lazarus.' So, when he heard that Lazarus was ill he hurried to them to heal Lazarus and to comfort them. That, at least, is what we would have expected, and later in the story some people asked why he didn't. But we are told:

'Jesus loved Martha and her sister and Lazarus. *So* when he heard that he was ill, he stayed two days longer in the place where he was.'

This was designed to make his miracle all the more impressive 'for the glory of God.'

Frankly, I find that thoroughly distasteful.

The story continues with the challenge to the two sisters to have faith, and then with the resurrection in all its gory detail – a detail designed to make the whole thing more believable, yet perhaps having the opposite effect.

So Lazarus is brought back from the dead and, apart from a couple of references in the immediate future, promptly disappears from history. It is difficult to see what else he could do. I summed up my own attitude to all of this a few years ago in a short poem:

What do we know about Lazarus?
He had two sisters
named Martha and Mary
and that's all there is to tell.

What do we know about Lazarus?
He died and was dead
for three days in tomb's bed
and that's all there is to tell.

What do we know about Lazarus?
Jesus called him out
with a life-giving shout
and that's all there is to tell.

What else do we know about Lazarus?
There isn't a thing,
not one single thing
and that's all there is to tell.

So why raise him
and not some other?
Yes, why raise him
and not my brother?

If miracles were really true
we'd have to say
that Jesus never learned
fair play!

But if the story is not true, where did it come from? We have seen the very human tendency to elaborate and magnify memories. You may remember a story told by Jesus about a rich man and a beggar called Lazarus where their situations are reversed after death (Luke 16:19–31). I suspect that that story was told many times and altered with the telling – perhaps Lazarus was raised to his new life in heaven by Jesus – and so it was gradually transformed until it became John's vehicle for the next great 'I am' claim of Jesus:

> 'I am the resurrection and the life; he who believes in me, though he die, yet shall he live, and whoever lives and believes in me shall never die.'

That is the Christian hope – not resurrection from death to life again like Lazarus, but resurrection to a new life in heaven. Belief in that kind of resurrection takes away the sting of death.

The story of the resurrection of Lazarus is intended to prove that Jesus has power over death. In due course the accounts of his own resurrection will attempt to prove the same thing.

45–54: This passage probably gives a pretty accurate account of the fears of the Jewish leaders and of their reasons for putting Jesus to death:

> 'If we let him go on thus, every one will believe in him, and the Romans will come and destroy both our holy place and our nation. . . it is expedient for you that one man should die for the people, and that the whole nation should not perish.' (vvs. 48 & 50)

But John turns this on its head when he says that Jesus will die 'not for the nation only, but to gather into one the children of God who are scattered abroad.' (v. 52)

Thus the crucifixion, the symbol of death, becomes the symbol of the triumph of Jesus through the growth of the church. I shall have more to say on this later on.

54–57: We are only half way through the Gospel, yet already John's story is beginning to build towards its climax as Jesus prepares to go to Jerusalem and to his death at the time of the Jewish Passover.

Chapter Twelve

Scholars identify all sorts of differences between the accounts of the end of the ministry of Jesus in the first three Gospels and John's account. These need not concern us for the most part.

1–8: This chapter includes a few final references to Lazarus but the real story is of Mary anointing the feet of Jesus in an expression of love and devotion.

Judas Iscariot criticised her extravagance. Here John demonises Judas as a hypocrite and a thief. We have no means of knowing whether he was right. Even if he was, it does not alter the criticisms I have made elsewhere of the relationship between Jesus and Judas – indeed it underpins one of them very forcibly. If Judas was the kind of man John claims, then Jesus slipped up badly in selecting him to be one of the twelve.

We shouldn't let this story pass without reference to some of its final words: 'The poor you always have with you.'

Whether through extravagant, emotional acts of generosity or through more considered, consistent generosity, we can all help to relieve poverty. But that is not enough. As members of a wealthy society where even the poorest can find food and drink, clothing and shelter, we should be striving for the eradication of poverty altogether.

For a brief period in the 20th century it really looked as though we were working towards that end, but then human greed was given political approval and encouragement, again leading the rich to become richer and the poor, poorer and to the financial chaos of the world as I write.

9–11: Here is a little note suggesting that Lazarus' fame put him in danger from the authorities and then in 12–19:

John explains the enthusiasm of the crowds for Jesus as down to the raising of Lazarus. You would think that such a remarkable event would have been heralded by all four Gospels but there isn't a hint of it in any of the others – so perhaps my unbelief is justified.

The other Gospels put the enthusiasm of the crowds down to the general success of his ministry in Galilee and to the normal excitement of crowds going to a festival.

20–26: In the early church there was considerable doubt about whether the Gospel was only for Jews or whether it was for everybody. This little passage is John's way of saying that it is for everybody.

27–36a: It is difficult to know what to make of this passage. Jesus clearly feels that he is going to his death and, as a young man, that fills him with anguish. But he feels that it is his destiny.

No one else has a clue what he is on about.

The theme of darkness and light is one which was taken from Isaiah (who is quoted later in this chapter). It clearly captured the imagination of John. There are times in many of our lives when we feel that we are walking 'in the darkness'. When we finally move into the light it comes as an exhilarating relief which sets us free.

There is no doubt that many find that exhilaration and freedom through Jesus and we should all be glad for them. But there are others of us who have only found our own path of light by breaking free from the institution that bears his name.

36b–43: This is a curious passage. John begins with those who 'did not believe' in Jesus and moves on to those who '*could not* believe' because God had 'blinded their eyes and hardened their heart lest they should see with their eyes and perceive with their heart.'

What a very strange God this is, one who actually doesn't want people to believe in him! Yet he is not even a very successful God, for in spite of all this 'many even of the authorities believed' in Jesus.

But they kept quiet about it 'lest they should be put out of the synagogue; for they loved the praise of men more than the praise of God.'

These last comments are very telling and speak to every generation. It is often so much easier and safer to keep our opinions to ourselves rather than to have the courage to stand out from the crowd and to stand up for what we believe to be right.

44–50: Jesus claims that those who believe in him and in his teaching are hearing and believing the word of God and so will avoid the final judgement of God.

Chapter Thirteen

1–20: The story of Jesus washing his disciples' feet is both well known and well loved in Christian circles. It is an acted parable demonstrating the fact that no one is so important that he is above giving service to others. In point of fact, there is no privilege in life greater than the privilege of service freely chosen and given.

I am not talking about slavery or serfdom or any other form of enforced service – or even ordinary employment. But to be able to choose to give your life, or a significant part of it, in the service of your fellow men and women is an immense privilege no matter how taxing and demanding it may often be.

21–30: John spells out the details of Judas' betrayal more fully than any of the other Gospels. He really has it in for Judas, and his dislike is evident. Was that dislike always there and was it mutual?

With that in mind have a look at verse 23 where we are told that 'one of his disciples, whom Jesus loved, was lying close to the breast of Jesus.' It is commonly believed that John was Jesus' favourite disciple, the one for whom he had a special love.

As human beings we all have our favourites – our 'best' friends – the people who mean most and matter most to us (although given our fickleness, they don't always remain 'best'!).

Having favourites is not an option open to God. To be a proper god he must love each of us in the same way and as much as our neighbour. He cannot have favourites which means that Jesus cannot be God!

In point of fact, the leader of a small bunch of men is very foolish to allow his preferences to become known. Having favourites leads to all sorts of friction and jealousy – as the Gospels themselves make clear. The twelve were the kind of petty, fractious, divided group, mostly of nonentities, that you can find in any human organisation. All of which means that Jesus was not only not-God, he wasn't even a very wise or sensible leader of men. And of course, with Judas he failed completely. Verse 30 is indescribably bleak: 'he immediately went out; and it was night.'

31–35: Jesus introduces a variant of the second commandment:

'Love one another, even as I have loved you. By this all men will know that you are my disciples, if you love one another.'

(vvs. 34–35)

Sadly, as anyone who has had any close acquaintance with the Christian church can tell you, it is no different from any other human institution. All the pettiness, jealousy, back-biting and squabbling that mark so many human institutions, where little people are seeking their own little bit of authority, status or glory, are to be found in the church just as vividly as anywhere else. There IS love to be found but that is true wherever we are. The church has no monopoly on love. It is just as common outside the church as within it.

157

36–38: If John was Jesus' favourite disciple, Simon Peter and his brother Andrew are two of mine.

Peter was so devoted and loyal but such a blunderer, always putting his foot in it, speaking out of turn and letting his enthusiasm get the better of him.

His brother Andrew was quite different. Modest and content that others should take the limelight and always ready to help others progress – with the result that he is hardly ever mentioned and I have no business mentioning him here!

Chapter Fourteen

Here is one of the most treasured passages in the whole of the New Testament.

For Christian believers it gives a real sense of assurance that after death they will enjoy a new life in heaven. In their gentle understated quiet way these words are spoken with such conviction that they are of immense power and comfort for those who wish to believe them.

They are not words to discuss or debate. They are words to believe or hope in. . . or not, as the case may be. For those of us with no belief in an afterlife and no desire for one, they are simply beautiful words, but where there can be no proof either way I hope that none of us would wish to undermine the hopes of others.

But what of that 'I am' claim in verse six, the climax of all these claims:

'I am the way, and the truth, and the life.'

Christians regard that as no more than a simple statement of fact. It seems to imply that there is no other way, no other truth and no other life worth talking about. To those of us who don't believe in Jesus it seems to be a breathtakingly arrogant and preposterous claim to make.

NO human teacher can show any of us 'the Way' let alone BE the way for us. Teachers can help, they can guide and they can inspire but in the end each of us has to find his or her own way. No one can do it for us.

The same can be said for Jesus' claim to be 'the truth'. No one can encapsulate the whole of truth, neither Jesus nor anyone else.

Truth may sometimes be absolute but it often seems to be relative. What is true for me may not be true for you. Pontius Pilate asked Jesus 'what is truth' and received no reply. Perhaps that is because there is no one reply and no final answer. We have to find what is true for ourselves and live by that truth.

And Jesus claimed to be 'the life'. In the context of this passage his claim is one of a life surmounting death – life in this life and life after death. Such a claim can neither be authenticated nor denied. The nearest we can come to examining it lies in examining the lives of his followers. Do they have some special quality which the rest of us lack?

After spending half of my life (so far) within the church I have no hesitation in saying that the answer is 'no'. That fact hit me while I was still in the church and living in India, where Christians were a small minority living amongst Hindus and Moslems. Christians are neither better nor worse than anybody else. There is nothing about them which marks them out from other people, nothing to suggest that there is any quality about their lives which others lack. And as for life after death: Hindus, Christians and Moslems all have their hopes or expectations concerning life after death. Who is to say whether any of them is right? As my mother used to say: 'All unknown the future lies. Let it rest.'

8–14: Jesus claims to be so at one with God that 'he who has seen me has seen the Father.' He asks his followers to believe, either because they have seen him or because they have seen the things he has done. And then he claims that his followers will do the same sort of things and even 'greater works than these will he do' through prayer and intercession.

It would be churlish to deny that both Jesus and his followers have done many wonderful things and achieved a very great deal. It is also true that a great deal of their achievement has been down to their Christianity. We should be thankful for all of these good things done in the name of Jesus.

We should be equally thankful for all of those good things done simply as a result of human curiosity, endeavour, invention and compassion no matter where their inspiration has come from.

15–31: Jesus goes on to speak of the way in which Christians will differ from their neighbours. The Holy Spirit will be given to enable them to continue his work and to give the comforting assurance that Jesus himself continues with them.

Once again, these are things which mean an immense amount to Christians. The Holy Spirit or the Spirit of Jesus is described as 'another Counsellor, to be with you for ever. . . the Spirit of truth.' He brings the companionship of Jesus himself.

Just as Jesus has been their teacher, guide and inspiration during his earthly ministry, so his Spirit, 'the Counsellor, the Holy Spirit' will be their teacher, guide and inspiration in the future. 'He will teach you all things, and bring to your remembrance all that I have said to you.' (v. 26)

In verse 17 we were told that those of us who are not Christians neither see the Spirit nor know him. That is perfectly true. To us, all this talk of the Spirit is just words. We have no means of verifying them except by what we see when we look at Christians and their behaviour. Frankly, we are not impressed.

But for many Christians the supreme importance of the Holy Spirit has barely been touched on except in the words 'I will not leave you desolate, I will come to you.' Now, in words which are intensely precious within the Christian community and which all of us can recognise as having extraordinary beauty, Jesus spells out one role of the Holy Spirit as Comforter:

> 'Peace I leave with you; my peace I give to you; not as the world gives do I give to you. Let not your hearts be troubled, neither let them be afraid.' (v. 27)

Forty years after I last used those words I am still moved by them. Words have a power of their own and there is no doubt that these words, spoken with sincerity and faith, have brought immense comfort to many people.

One of my brothers once told me that he thought it was the language of the Bible and of Christian worship which kept me within the Christian community for so long. Certainly, as an unbelieving celebrant, these words have continued to resonate with me. I spend so much of my time with people who have just been bereaved. I want to bring to them a measure of peace, both through my approach to them and also through the words I choose to use in funeral ceremonies. The right words, carefully chosen and spoken with simple honesty and integrity, can bring precisely the same kind of comfort that those lovely words of verse 27 bring to Christians.

The chapter ends with Jesus claiming that his time is up, that he is doing what God has commanded him and that his destiny is not in the hands of those who will condemn and kill him, but of God.

Chapter Fifteen

1–11: Here is yet another 'I am' claim and for once I have no quarrel with it. This image of Jesus as the true vine and his disciples as the branches which need pruning from time to time, in order to bear fruit, is a valuable one.

We all have roots in the teachings and examples of our childhood and youth. If we are to bear good fruit in our adult lives, the teachings themselves need to be examined, purified and pruned. The examples set before us need to be examined too. There are times when they will inspire us and there are times when they will be found wanting.

Our examination and sifting of these things will be part of our growing up whether it happens in our teens and twenties or in our forties or eighties. We go on questing, testing, pruning, learning, and as a result, hopefully, in each of our lives we manage to produce some good fruit.

12–17: Jesus reiterates his commandment of love – here in the sense of friendship. His disciples have become his friends. They are to love one another as he has loved them and to be prepared to sacrifice their lives for one another.

Epicurus was another great teacher who focussed on the importance of friendship – ordinary, simple human friendship.

Few of us are prepared to go as far as Jesus asks. Thankfully few of us are ever put in a position where our friendship is tested in such extreme ways. But there is no doubt that ordinary human friendship, freely given and gladly received, is one of the fundamental foundations on which decent human life is built – one of the foundations which can lead to happiness in human life.

18–27: Sadly, here Jesus spells out the way in which Christians go wrong – and not just Christians. Jews before them, and for ever since, have gone wrong in similar ways. And many other religious people follow the same path. It always leads to dislike, distaste and disapproval and it sometimes leads to persecution.

In many religions there is an assumption that 'we are right and

161

h

everyone else is wrong'; 'we have the Truth and everyone else is living in error'; 'we follow the path of virtue and everyone else is mired in sin'. These attitudes give religious people a sense of superiority. 'God I thank thee that I am not as other men are.' And it leads them to be evangelistic.

This is supremely a religious problem but it is not solely a religious problem. You can find it in modern humanist groups. And you can find it very powerfully in imperialist nations. It was once a very British vice and we are not wholly free from it yet. It is certainly a current American vice. In this country my generation was still being brought up to it – not, I think, wholly consciously. Because of the Empire and the British Navy; and because of our Protestant Christian ethic (not to speak of our wealth!); we were superior to anybody else and always in the right.

This insistence on being different; the spoken or implied claim to superiority; the claim that we are right and everybody else is wrong, sinful or at very least, inadequate – these are the things that divide us from one another and spoil human relationships and society. They lead to dislike, hatred, persecution – yes, and terrorism too.

We need to wake up to the fact that we are all only human beings after all, all of us fallible but muddling through to the best of our ability. And if we can muddle through in a spirit of friendship and mutual support, we shall find life very much easier and happier.

Chapter Sixteen

1–4a: Jesus underlines the fact that Christians can expect to be expelled from Judaism and also persecuted.

4b–15: He reiterates his promise that the Holy Spirit will come to his disciples and will 'convince the world of sin and of righteousness and of judgement. . .' He will also 'guide you into all the truth.' (vvs. 8 & 13)

My attitudes to most of this will need no more spelling out here, but verse 13 is important. It involves the recognition that the teaching of Jesus on its own is not enough. So often religion – not just the Christian religion – looks back to ancient teachers as if it was only in ancient times that proper teaching about human life can be found. I have done this myself – indeed, in a sense I am doing it now!

But there are many ethical questions facing us today which the ancients never dreamed of; many life-problems they could never foresee. Christians would say that the Holy Spirit will guide into all truth but to an outsider things don't seem to work that way. The Christian church often seems either to set its face against new truth, or to spend its time playing catch up when society has moved on from old entrenched positions.

We all need to cultivate an openness to new ideas and new thinking – not an uncritical openness, but an openness nonetheless.

16–24: Jesus talks of his forthcoming death and resurrection in terms of a birth into new life, but most of what he is saying goes over his disciples' heads. Did they manage to cotton on to the fact that grief lay ahead with the promise of joy to follow their sorrow?

25–33: Here is a curiosity: Jesus tells his disciples that he will no longer pray for them because God loves them. If that is the case, why did he ever need to pray for them. Didn't God always love them?

In fact, since by definition God knows everything, why is there ever any need to put him in the picture and to ask for the things we think we need?

I have one or two vague memories of Christian answers to such questions but I never did find them very satisfying.

For no apparent reason the disciples suddenly seem to feel that they know what Jesus is talking about and it leads to a reaffirmation of their faith. That in turn leads Jesus to warn that they will all run away, leaving him alone. But he will not be totally alone because God will be with him.

Verse 33 means a great deal to Christians and not without good cause. Whatever we think of Christianity, the crucifixion didn't put an end to the ministry of Jesus. On the contrary, it led to the teaching of Jesus becoming known throughout much of the world. In that sense Christians have every cause to claim that Jesus has overcome, giving them ample reason for 'good cheer'.

And now, having said that he will no longer pray for his disciples, he proceeds in chapter seventeen to do just that!

Chapter Seventeen

In the opening part of this chapter Jesus stresses the fact that his whole ministry has been aimed at showing God to the world and speaking the words of God to the world. And again and again he stresses his own perfect unity with God 'the Father'.

He stresses that his prayer is only for his own, and not for the rest of us. It is for his own at that time but it is also for his future disciples.

Once again he points out that Christians are different from the rest of us. 'They are not of the world, even as I am not of the world.' (v. 16) I have said quite enough on that subject.

But the main thrust of the prayer is repeated over and over again. He prays that his disciples 'may be one, even as we are one. . . that they may all be one. . . that they may be one even as we are one, I in them and thou in me, that they may become perfectly one.'

As a Christian that prayer haunted me because it didn't happen and it hasn't happened. During my own time within the church there was a serious attempt to re-unite two fragments of the church but it failed.

Although, at the time, I could and did justify our separation, in the end the prayer of Jesus seemed more important than all our reasons for separation.

But the significant thing here is that God has not managed to persuade Christians to live together in harmony and peace and love in spite of the prayer of Jesus. That is a devastating indictment of Christians and it doesn't say much for the authority and power of their God either. It is no wonder that even when 'the world' respects Jesus it has so little time for his church.

Chapter Eighteen

1–14: Jesus clearly had a 'presence' which enabled him to overawe hostile crowds and pass through them safely. John Wesley cultivated the same ability. But this time Jesus allowed himself to be taken.

The moment of bathos, mentioned in other Gospels, when

Peter draws his sword is mentioned again but this time there is no mention of Jesus healing the high priest's slave.

15–27: The story of the beginning of the trial of Jesus is told together with the story of the denials of Peter. But there is also a little personal note saying 'I was there' because I 'was known to the high priest'. There is no mention of this in the other Gospels.

28–40: Jesus is brought before Pilate, accused of claiming to be 'the King of the Jews'. As the Roman governor, Pilate alone had the authority to put Jesus to death.

Jesus claims that his 'kingship is not of this world' and that he has 'come into the world to bear witness to the truth.' (vvs. 36–37)

But when Pilate asks 'what is truth' he receives no answer at all. Christians dismiss Pilate's question and never consider it to be serious. Whether or not they were right to do so: whether the question WAS a serious one, it IS a serious question. Christians would claim that the ministry and teaching of Jesus answer the question, but right from being a lad I have been bothered that Jesus gave Pilate no answer.

Pilate declared Jesus' innocence but gave way to the Jewish authorities' wish that he should be put to death. Whether we think of that as weakness or political wisdom will depend on our reading of the situation he was in. His decision was certainly morally wrong.

Chapter Nineteen

1–16: I do not need to dwell on the nastiness or hypocrisy concentrated in these verses. Whilst human beings normally seem to be pretty decent there is no doubt that we are capable of being pretty vile, especially when we are given a little bit of authority. No one comes out of this with any credit, least of all the chief priests who finally cry, 'We have no king but Caesar'. To their fellow Jews that kind of hypocritical abasement was utterly despicable.

17–22: At the crucifixion Pilate mocked the priests by adding a placard to the cross of Jesus saying, 'The King of the Jews'.

23–27: Some of the female disciples attended the crucifixion as did John. Jesus placed his mother in John's care. Given the fact of his brothers and sisters, that seems strange. Perhaps by this time there was too great a rift between Jesus and his siblings. Previously they have always been with his mother when she has come to see Jesus but here they are not mentioned.

28–42: The death and burial of Jesus.

Each of the Gospels records words of Jesus from the cross. John's are recorded nowhere else.

The burial is significant because two fairly well-known citizens come out of the closet and let their approval of Jesus be known.

Chapter Twenty

1–10: Mary Magdalene, Peter and 'the disciple Jesus loved' (normally taken to be John) visit the empty tomb and find the folded grave-clothes. If this is an accurate picture of what really happened it demolishes my theory from Matthew that the earthquake, not mentioned here, swallowed the body.

There is no sign in this Gospel of the devastating natural phenomena mentioned by Matthew. If John had stopped his account at verse 10 I would have been inclined to accept his simple, sober account of what happened. But he didn't.

11–18: The disciples leave and Mary stays. She sees two angels in the tomb. Why did Peter and John not see them? Then she sees Jesus but doesn't recognise him. Why not?

Jesus says 'Do not hold me' as if there is something peculiar about his risen body, yet a week later he is telling Thomas to place his hands in his wounded side.

19–23: Having been seen by Mary, Jesus now enters a closed room and shows himself to some of his disciples. He gives them his peace, tells them that he is sending them out to continue his ministry, gives them the Holy Spirit (in a fashion far removed from Luke's story in the Acts of the Apostles), and tells them that they have the power to forgive (or not to forgive) people's sins.

It all sounds a rather pat summary.

24–30: Not surprisingly the absentee Thomas doesn't believe his fellows so Jesus appears again and convinces him saying, 'Have you believed because you have seen me? Blessed are those who have not seen and believed.' (v. 29)

John ends the chapter by spelling out why he has written his Gospel: 'that you may believe that Jesus is the Christ, the Son of

God, and that believing you may have life in his name.' (v. 312)

That sounds like the end of the Gospel, but there is a post-script:

Chapter Twenty-one

1–14: After a night's fishing the disciples find Jesus on the beach and have breakfast with him.

15–19: And then comes the famous reinstatement of Simon Peter. Three times Peter had denied that he was a follower of Jesus. Now, three times, he is required to profess his allegiance all over again. This seems to me to be both unnecessary and unkind. It is no wonder that Peter was upset.

20–25: Here a hint of the old jealousies rears its head. What has Jesus in store for John, his favourite? 'That's my business', says Jesus – and on that elevated note the story ends.

Note on the Resurrection

As a young man I had no problem with the resurrection and no doubts about it. I didn't believe on the basis of the evidence. As we have seen, much of the evidence is suspect anyway. I believed because I had been brought up to believe. Why would I question those who had served me so well in so many other respects?

It took a major crisis in my life to enable me to discover where my own thinking led me. That thinking led first to the rejection of the whole concept of miracle and then, inevitably, to the rejection of the miracles of the incarnation (the birth of Jesus) and the resurrection.

But there did seem to be one evidence for the resurrection which I had not considered and which could not be brushed aside – namely, the existence of the church. If Jesus did not rise from the dead, how can you explain the existence of the Christian church?

At first sight that seems unanswerable and it bothered me for a long time. But then I looked again at the other major religions and some of the more successful modern sects – looked at them and lectured on them.

The foundations of many of them are extraordinarily fragile. They range from unbelievable to suspect, to possibly or probably fraudulent, to fantastic! I began to feel that, given the right conditions, virtually any kind of religion could be successful. So what are the right conditions?

1. A gap in the market.
2. A group of convinced, enthusiastic salesmen
   or missionaries.
3. Organisational or business skills.

1. When Jesus died there was a gap in the market throughout the whole of Europe. There was widespread cynicism concerning the old gods. If Judaism had not been tied so firmly to the Jewish nation it could have swept the board. Instead, when a sect of Judaism which was not tied to the Jewish nation came along, it did sweep the board.

2. It did so because, at its heart, there was a convinced sales-force. Although I don't believe in the resurrection, I'm sure that they did – beginning (after the twelve) with the apostle Paul.

3. As the movement spread, those with organisational skills began to take over, just as when small businesses grow, accountants and lawyers begin to move in.

4. But Christianity stumbled on a fourth road to success. After 300 years of growth like the mustard seed of Jesus' parable, they achieved political power.

It transformed the church which now became an instrument of state. Success was now guaranteed but the price has always been too high. The teaching of Jesus was fatally compromised and ever since the church has pursued the twin goals of power and wealth.

The teaching of Jesus HAS survived but only because, in every generation there have been those who focussed upon it and tried to live their lives according to 'the way' it expounds. That 'way' has much to teach us all. It doesn't matter what our religion or lack of it, the teaching of Jesus really does contain a great deal that is of permanent value. I hope that this book of mine, for all its criticisms, has shown that. I hope that it will enable some or even many people who are not Christians to find their way through the minefield of the Gospels while collecting a fine bunch of flowers on the way.

The Gospels contain much that is irrelevant and much that is dreadful and plain wrong. But they also contain teaching of rare quality. All of us will benefit from the study of that teaching.